C0-DMX-070

```
P          Erwin, Robert.
41
.E7        The great language
1990         panic and other
             essays in cultural
             history.
```

$19.95

DATE			
SEP 1995			

CHICAGO PUBLIC LIBRARY
PULLMAN BRANCH
11001 S. INDIANA AVE. 60628

© THE BAKER & TAYLOR CO.

The Great Language Panic

The Great Language Panic and Other Essays in Cultural History

Robert Erwin

The University of Georgia Press • Athens and London

© 1990 by Robert Erwin
Published by the University of Georgia Press
Athens, Georgia 30602
All rights reserved
Designed by Mary Mendell
Set in Palatino
The paper in this book meets the guidelines for
permanence and durability of the Committee on
Production Guidelines for Book Longevity of the
Council on Library Resources.

Printed in the United States of America
94 93 92 91 90   5 4 3 2 1
Library of Congress Cataloging in Publication Data
Erwin, Robert.
The great language panic and other essays in cultural
history / Robert Erwin.
p. cm.
ISBN 0-8203-1211-8 (alk. paper)
1. Language and history.   I. Title.
P41.E7   1990
400—dc20   89-20329 CIP
British Library Cataloging in Publication Data available

In Memory of W.A.E.
a hunter who put me on the track of history

Contents

Acknowledgments ix

Shoulder to Shoulder Against the Middle-Aged: A Preface 1

The Mesopotamian Connection 11

Feudalism: We Should Be So Lucky 25

Heresy 41

Yes and No: The Sociology of Intellectuals 53

The Great Language Panic 66

Reform from Below 81

Fenimore Cooper and the Invention of Writing 95

The Village Apollo 107

The Case of the Missing T-Shirt 117

Lifestyle 130

Index 143

Acknowledgments

For publishing preliminary versions of the essays in this book, I thank the editors and former editors of the following periodicals: *American Scholar, Antioch Review, Christian Century, Harvard Magazine, Helicon Nine, Politics and Society, Public Policy,* and *Virginia Quarterly Review.*

Over the years other articles have gone through the mill at other periodicals, and from the experience as a whole two editors stand out in my mind, not only in relief but as a relief. Gloria Vando Hickok, founder and editor of *Helicon Nine*, a magazine about women in the arts, is one. Her husband, the builder and conservationist Bill Hickok, is a lifelong friend, and so I know her well. If this were a purely personal note, I would tell you what a demon she is at playing the Dictionary Game. For writers, however, at least for this writer, the point about Gloria is openness. On good days she views the literary universe as akin to the true universe, a place with room for everything, and she is willing to try it all. Of course any number of magazine editors scan the horizon more intensely than Gloria—spotting trends, divining the coming topics and the coming formulas, balancing the new against the established. But their search is the opposite of openness. It is more like the opportunism of market researchers and commodity traders. Manuscripts are not engaged on their own terms. They are sifted for utility in exploiting a niche.

The other editor I have in mind is Robert Fogarty of *Antioch Review*. Him I don't know well. Our dealings have been strictly business. Yet I notice he prefers not just most of the sentences but all the sentences to be comprehensible, and his concern is rare. So many editors, once they get the gist of a text and decide it suits the mix they are after, want to move on immediately—drum up another project, exert charm, manage, or go home for dinner. If necessary, Ms. Stein in the back room can read the words consecutively later.

Obviously I did not myself uncover from original sources and numerous languages most of the quotations and information presented here. I am indebted to a host of scholars, through their published work, for that. They deserve credit. But this is a book of historical interpretation, not research. Style is paramount, and that rules out footnotes. What to do? The answer to the problem, it occurs to me, is to slip citations into these Acknowledgments—at one and the same time a bravura stylistic ploy and a way of owning up to some of my debts.

Actually that is not as wacky as it sounds. The books named below constitute neither a comprehensive reading list nor a ranking for authoritativeness. Some I barely drew upon in a direct way. Rather, with respect to certain subjects, they happened to be the point where I washed ashore, from which I explored inland, to which I returned to think about what I found.

A. Leo Oppenheim's *Ancient Mesopotamia* was my beachhead for entering Akkadian civilization. David Herlihy's *Medieval Households* and Edward Peters's *Heresy and Authority in Medieval Europe* helped me to expand and consolidate ideas on feudalism and spiritual monopoly. I. F. Stone's *The Trial of Socrates* confirmed a number of intuitions about the social role of intellectuals. Stanley Rosen's *The Limits of Analysis*, though it says little about language per se, came to hand at just the time to crystalize reflections on transcending language through language. Exploring the life and work of Fenimore Cooper caused me to reread Henry Nash Smith's *Virgin Land*, a worthwhile exercise that I would probably not have got round to. I wrote on lifestyle mostly as a "participant-observer," but the piece led me to an interesting book I might otherwise have missed, Frances Fitzgerald's *Cities on a Hill*. Thoreau advised us not to judge a man till we walked a mile in his moccasins. For tracking Thoreau himself—a disillusioning experience —I found Richard Lebeaux's *Young Man Thoreau* indispensable.

Whatever I know in general about doing history, as J. H. Hexter calls it, comes from hanging around with historians during my years as a university-press editor. By osmosis, I learned a lot from Edward Peters and Bruce Kuklick at the University of Pennsylvania, from Robert Rotberg when we were at Harvard, and from Daniel Boorstin and William Leuchtenburg long ago as a junior editor at the University of Chicago.

Lastly a hurrah for intelligent conversation. There is no better stimulus, solace, test laboratory, and excuse for not working. While I was rewriting the essays in this collection, frequent lunches with Joseph Boskin, who had just finished a book himself, *Sambo: The Rise and Demise of an American Jester*, served all those purposes admirably. Too bad we didn't tape our conversations and benefit posterity with the Linguine Papers. I am grateful also to Elizabeth Badger, who more than once managed to say what I needed to hear and what I wanted to hear in the same conversation.

The Great Language Panic

Shoulder to Shoulder Against the Middle-Aged

A Preface

Years ago at the University of Chicago Press I shared an office for a while with Mitford Mathews, Professorial Lecturer in Linguistics in his faculty capacity, author of *A Dictionary of Americanisms* for the press, and by then on the brink of retirement. Thinking back, I try to recall how a junior editor and an elderly lexicographer ended up in the same room, whether we got on each other's nerves, and what came of the experience.

To an office manager the combination might seem reasonable. The press was prospering, adding staff, running out of space in its old brick building. Somebody had to double up, and as an apprentice I couldn't expect a private office. I was happy just to be started in the profession I wanted, and I felt privileged to tidy up the solecisms and misspellings of real live authors. The writers I knew personally then —among them Philip Roth, the poet David Ray, a bartender named Jack who loved Hemingway—were barely published or never to be published.

For Mathews the case was more complicated. As the last salaried person in a small dictionary department being phased out by the press, he had long standing but little future. His academic appointment was running out too, and he approached mandatory retirement age at the end of an era when that usually meant instant amputation— no more courses, no more office and mailbox. A few years would pass yet before the national rise in enrollment and the increase in grants to colleges allowed a large number of older scholars to continue teaching and research indefinitely, if not at their home universities then at the new branch campuses that had to assemble faculties overnight.

Here appears the fine hand of a canny publisher, Roger Shugg, who directed the University of Chicago Press with great success at the time. The crush to fit x bodies into y space may have prompted Roger to dissolve the dictionary department sooner rather than later, but Roger was never a man to do things for just one reason. He loved to spread his bets and angle for multiple payoffs. He had a genius for hiring people with what I called adjoining talents. If they liked each other, good ensemble work resulted. If they became rivals, he channeled their competition into performance. If one left for another job, the other covered. In a single year without missing a beat we took a turnover of nine people who had seemed to me indispensable.

Regarding M's situation, a run-of-the-mill press director might have searched for special support from the university administration or outside sources, but at Mathews's age that would have meant waiting months or years better spent revising *A Dictionary of Americanisms*, pretty much a one-man production. Having satisfied himself that M was keen to revamp and extend the *Dictionary*, which had made money for the press in its first edition, Roger kept him at work in our building under a formula that saved face for everyone by casting the arrangement as an exchange of favors between author and publisher. Somewhere at the back of Roger's mind, I imagine, was the ancillary thought that proximity to a young man from the main enterprise might help to keep M from dawdling over the revision.

So far it all sounds boringly practical, and indeed our work routines, mine and M's, meshed. We both needed quiet, and neither of us used the telephone more than two or three times a day. Except for a part-time assistant, a graduate student who worked out of a carrel in the library, M rarely had visitors. When I needed to see others at the press, I went to their offices. Most of the time I was copyediting a book to be published next season and reading proofs of another. Behind my littered desk were a couple of shelves with duplicate files and some reference books and manuals, and sometimes three or four manuscripts in folders were stacked on my typewriter. (The janitors followed a classic publishing rule: never remove anything except from a wastebasket.) These manuscripts were passed along for evaluation by the managing editor, Alex Morin, and they were probably the weakest candidates in the slush pile, but I tried to approach each one with the concentration and impartiality of an ideal Supreme Court judge. It was obvious that I should occupy the smaller part of the office, for M —singlehandedly revising a dictionary in the days before Xerox machines, word processors, portable microreaders, and the like—set out numerous metal trays full of index cards in an exact order on heavy work tables, and he had a bank of file cabinets as well, packed with correspondence, notes, source material, and drafts. This equipment and his oversize desk dominated the room, nicely symbolizing his seniority, to some equivalent of which I presumably should aspire in due course in my sphere, whatever that turned out to be.

Members of the class of 1970 (let alone 1990), already disturbed by the thought of a world without copy machines, will recoil when they hear that parcel services were lacking too at this point in the 1950s. The telephone and the end of mass immigration had made office boys and messengers scarce a generation earlier, Railway Express was fading, and the carriers who currently send your package to many distant cities overnight did not exist. Even oil companies and downtown law firms used messengers sparingly, and only emergencies could lead a university press into such extravagance. A few times a year, however, someone at our press would phone an outfit called Flash Delivery, and I would enjoy the arrival under my window of their man on a motorcycle with a sidecar. The man from Flash dressed like a Brando hoodlum—boots, leather jacket, jeans, and menacing belt buckle— but he had the pale skin and abstracted look of a rabbinical student. I named him Lucifer behind his back.

Notice that I said "under my window." We each had one, which could be opened and closed as we pleased and showed us a big piece of sky as well as Lucifer—worth more than a word processor any day. The decor of the office I shared with M was Basic Piano Factory overlaid with South Side soot from furnaces that burned soft coal from the mines of downstate Illinois. Our furniture—ugly yellow oak—was chipped, marred, nicked, gouged, and stained, and the ashtrays were green glass. Yet the place had its strong points. Thick walls kept out street noise and all the clatter in the building. The door was a beauty, the whole wide heart of a tree, hung by a turn-of-the-century craftsman to a tolerance of about a sixty-fourth of an inch. We sat far enough from one another to work undisturbed by sniffling and pencil tapping but close enough to read funny items back and forth as we came across them in our respective lines of work. A huffy letter of complaint from a Germanic author provided the immortal claim "I believe to possess exellent knowledge of English." M's *Dictionary* was compiled on historical principles—meaning among other things that the earliest known printed use of a term figured in each entry—and had attracted a scattering of volunteer correspondents. A British army officer, as I recall of what was read to me, doubtless a champion worker of crossword puzzles, was overcome with emotion upon discovering in an old American book an earlier occurrence of an expression hitherto associated with Davy Crockett.

But did we really get along? Given the shock of aging and retirement, M had every right to be touchy. God knows what the scholars of his generation lived on when the time came. They had put in a fair number of years at antique wages and most of the rest in a period of depression and wartime controls. For a courtly old gent who had grown up in warmer parts, Hyde Park (the University of Chicago neighborhood) seemed to me a bad place in which to be "severed." It was dirty, piercing cold half the year, surrounded by slums, and intellectually trendy. I can't believe that Mrs. M, plump and white-haired as I remember, still felt at home there. The vogue then was for cool, geometric, buttoned-up things, but M's apartment was full of floppy plants. Who was left that had welcomed the Mathewses as a promising young couple in a more gemütlich neighborhood and overlapped with them in their prime? I don't think that M cared to talk about losses and disappointments with graduate students he had turned out over the years. These men (and a handful of women) were now thirty-five years old or so, scattered, preoccupied with their own careers in fields of linguistics different from the philology in which he had been trained.

Whether M was touchy or not, I might have blanked him out, making the situation slightly more uncomfortable for him and guaranteeing that I would get nothing from it. Like most Americans, I had been exposed to the message that anyone with wrinkles should play minor character parts only. Given that misdirection and given the jazzbo extracurricular phase I was in at the time, how could I take seriously an "Americanist" who didn't know Charlie Parker from Dizzy Gillespie?

As it turned out, though, Roger was right in his hunch, the capstone of this particular scheme, that the generations would stimulate each other. If M felt angry or lost, he never let on to me. He beat me to the office in the morning. He talked more about today's work and tomorrow's plans than about the past. He patiently listened to me expound a half-baked analogy between Parker and Mozart, and I was charmed by an ancient green eyeshade he sometimes wore.

It was good for a young person starting out in one branch of the word business to witness an old-timer still going at it in his own branch with zest and skill. I watched him cheerfully inserting new citations of first occurrence in place of some he thought he had nailed down forever. I saw him happily rewriting entries to accommodate newly uncovered variant meanings. It was good for him to see someone from the future taking a path roughly related to his, someone who would remember him as a presence rather than a name in a footnote.

I do indeed remember Mitford Mathews in action, and I honor him for his lessons in language as performance. When the revision was finished and his trays went into storage and the time came for him to leave, he gave me a pair of scissors used in the making of the *Oxford English Dictionary*, which he had worked on several summers long ago. At that age I was afraid to be sentimental, but the scissors grew on me as I carried them to the offices and jobs that followed, talisman as well as keepsake.

If any influence remains so long after we stood shoulder to shoulder against the middle-aged on Ellis Avenue, I suppose there must be a trace of M's thinking in my aversion to temporal provincialism, a conspicuous feature of this book. Overestimating newness plus trivializing the past equals temporal provincialism. All the essays presented here try to rise above the hick outlook that comes from living perpetually in a little crossroads called the present. For people with disposable income, just plain provincialism is not what it used to be. An estimated quarter-million Westerners have visited Nepal in recent years, and Harvard Yard swarms with Japanese tourists. Yet temporal provincialism persists. The past is regarded as optional—okay in bits and pieces for entertainment, sentiment and fantasy, propaganda, selective extrapolation, and scholastic exercises if there is time to spare but peripheral to "real" life. In truth, of course, the past was neither more nor less real than the present, but the sheer range and accumulation of experience there, the abundance of completed patterns, make it a cosmopolitan place. To assume otherwise amounts to temporal provincialism, as boorish as the regular kind.

There may be a trace of M too in my concern with how language carries out cultural instructions. History and language openly intersect. People have heard of a celebrity named Cleopatra. They have seen Clint Eastwood win the West with eight shots from his six-shooter. They perceive that they are somewhat younger than their parents. It is more difficult to bring consciousness of culture into speech, however. In all the clever words lavished in the controversy over prescriptive versus descriptive grammar when *Webster's Third New International Dictionary* was published, for instance, virtually nothing was said about the American preference for framing two components of a single subject in a competitive, adversarial way and how typical that way of framing is of our way of representing the world. Statistics, polls, "behavior," yes. The number of viewers who watch which programs will be tabulated tonight while the TV sets are still warm. Not one person in a thousand, though, will wonder about the phenomenon of watching as such or the phenomenon of responding to pollsters among the possibilities of human action. Philip Slater is entitled to poetic license in *The Pursuit of Loneliness* when he says that the American ideal is to make meaningful contact unnecessary in daily life. *Leave it on the answering machine. Doing my thing. Personal growth.* Unison of belief in individualism nevertheless resembles any other collective value. A shared ideal of individualism, a nationally organized apparatus for solitude, is still shared. There is such a thing as conforming to tradition by claiming not to be governed by tradition. In one of the essays that follow, "Fenimore Cooper and the Invention of Writing," I argue that the social provision for novelists remains much the same as it was five generations ago. Indeed, since all the essays here focus on the meaning of a word or emblematic name, I try in all of them to make culture visible. Like gestalt drawings in which light areas and dark areas alternate as foreground and background, depending on how you look at them, language is embedded in culture as culture is embedded in language.

What undoubtedly has a bearing on this book is M's zest for language, sustained from start to finish. On the face of it, a retiring old man may seem a strange choice to set the example. Besides, except in cases of overwhelming affliction, why is staying attentive to language special?

I grant practically unlimited and nonstop incentives, positive and negative, to pay attention. The satisfaction, even the illusion, of getting across in close relations is consuming. At the public level too the satisfaction is great. The Irish writer Frank O'Connor once said to an interviewer that at some point in composing a story he liked the characters to stand on their own feet and tell him to go to hell. In a sense this animation of a verbal structure amounted to nothing more than the superstitions and pep talks by which athletes pump themselves up for a contest—the ball player who won't change socks during a hitting streak. Yet O'Connor's sense of confirmation, of moving with the grain of the world, is how right moments with language feel. Furthermore, to find words to advance one's interests is crucial, coupled with the need to interpret accurately the words of those with power to harm or gull.

Wrestling with formalities of language can be absorbing. Columnists such as William Safire who police our diction provide a bit of fun and drama as they chase after buzzwords and barbarisms that create a public nuisance. Their sometime opponents the sociolinguists, like welfare workers sympathetic to the verbal underclass, discover patterns of language much too effective and intricate to be labeled "substandard." Whoever falls under the spell of master arbiters of usage is hooked on the pleasures of taste. (At the time I shared an office with M, I would, because of what H. W. Fowler wrote, sooner have taken a beating than use "due to" as a compound preposition.)

Moving up the scale of abstraction, substantive arguments over words are a staple of intellectual excitement. We know that people will kill over a term such as *transubstantiation*, and even in humdrum settings the arguments go on forever. Words such as *freedom, love*, and *reason* get set up in the piazza, where we circle around them for centuries, regarding them from every angle in every light. Half the people crossing the piazza are squabbling about other words as they go. Who is a "victim" and who is a "criminal"? Is "progress" an exhausted concept or still potentially a basis for worthwhile action? What does "mind" consist of? Et cetera.

Modern philosophers raised the stakes by introducing a global distrust of language without suggesting a workable substitute. Through philosophies of language formulated over the past hundred years or more run desperate subtexts: opaqueness and relativity block our view of the universe; we will scorch the countryside and sell our lives dearly against tautologies and unverifiable expressions. Images of a retreat to a grim island fortress, formed when I sampled logical positivism about the time I knew Mathews, popped out of my subconscious years later in the course of writing "The Great Language Panic," another of the essays that follow.

Granted that language attracts and alarms, unites and divides, serves and bemuses. Granted that our brains, for better or worse, are probably "wired" for language. The fact remains that from time to time everyone tunes out. The volume of words to which we are exposed is crushing. Formalities grow tedious. Handling utterances on which our interests hinge is nerve-wracking. The compounding of nonverbal pressures through the exploitative streak in language can drive us to jam words together in desperation or to go blank, just as in self-defense we walk city streets without really seeing the buildings that dwarf us.

A few years after M and I parted, I began to write essays (in addition to stories and other kinds of articles). While I worked at finding the range, so to speak, I realized that M's immunity to language burnout, to going numb or falling asleep over words and names, was rare. Frequently the blanking out lasts so long and spreads so widely that the use of a particular word or name gets wildly out of alignment with any possible meaning. Without any intention of irony or metaphor, for instance, we throw a word such as *feudalism* around almost at random, referring to a scarcity of lipstick in China as "feudal." If a particular cluster of values matters—say independence, love of nature, and plain living—then the supposed embodiment matters. Hence it bears thinking about if Thoreau, one of the subjects here, was a freeloader who prized literary success over a sunrise every time. If a given word is likely to provoke action, we ought to be clear what kind of action we summon when we pronounce it. "Reform," the subject of another essay, conventionally stands for moderate change in contrast to "radicalism." In practice, however, perhaps reform entails cruelty and double-dealing. I was and continue to be drawn to write about cases of misalignment—the common denominator of the essays presented here.

Though few of us develop M's stamina, nearly all of us have moments in which we wake up, in which certain words and names register as though for the first time. And no wonder. Life without meaning is unendurable in the same way that life without body fluids is unsustainable, not because this state of affairs is inevitable or preferable but because it happens to be the case. The best hope of limiting the common quotient of misalignments is to share the work. Whoever comes alive to a word ought to hold it to the light for the rest of us to notice.

Although I would not want to blame my habits on M, one additional characteristic of the book that follows seems to me to reflect his spirit. Preliminary versions of the essays presented here were earlier published in various periodicals, but, contrary to the more common practice of reprinting essays verbatim, I have treated the text of every one of them as first draft.

There are good reasons why authors frequently let their shorter pieces be gathered unrevised. They may be involved in new work which they consider better and more important. They may have a sporting mentality: if they once thought something worth publishing, they are honor-bound to stand by it, just as an athlete must stand by the game he or she played on a given day of the season.

I wouldn't be surprised if there are bad reasons as well, but my decision to rewrite these essays is no reflection on ordinary practice. I simply found that on every topic I had more to say. Sometimes the impetus came from new research and writing by others. Sometimes it came from comments by readers (friendly, critical, friendly *and* critical). Sometimes just from living with a topic longer—getting past the first date.

Whether the effort of revision was worthwhile need not worry anyone but me. What matters for readers is what they now get out of the chapters individually and as an ensemble. Tough odds to figure. Readers tend to read better than writers write, and so what chance does a text have in this cruel world? On the other hand, if they are so disposed readers can make just about any book sail like a kite.

The Mesopotamian Connection

Probably more linguistic and cultural diversity existed fifteen thousand years ago than now. Among widely dispersed hunters and gatherers with scant knowledge of neighboring bands and no knowledge at all of the rest of the world, each cluster of encampments was in effect occupied by a distinct people carrying on yet another experiment in language and social patterns. As late as 1938 first contact was made with a group nearly fifty thousand strong who were unaware of other societies, the Dani of New Guinea.

The so-called neolithic revolution—which introduced domesticated plants and animals, plowing and irrigation, metallurgy, more effective methods of food storage, sail-driven and pack-animal transport (in some cases with the addition of the wheel), and improved building techniques—of course altered the situation for the greater part of humankind. A powerful feedback loop of population growth, material gain, and innovation through contact formed.

About five thousand years ago the resources and stimuli generated in this way served as the foundation for civilization, an organizational revolution. This further development was marked by the invention of writing, sophisticated measurement and bureaucracy, population massed in cities and mobilized for sustained military campaigns or public works, intense craft specialization, and the extension of war, trade, diplomacy, and the exchange of knowledge over long distances. For the first time rulers could more or less expect plans, directives, and administration to go forward without their personal presence.

It goes almost without saying that these developments, which sound so orderly and irresistible in anthropology textbooks, occurred unevenly and incompletely at any given place or time. Evidence from skeletons in the burial grounds suggests, for example, that some proto-civilized mound builders of the Mississippi Valley had a lower standard of nutrition than their paleolithic forebears, perhaps because they squandered more than they could afford on religious observances and artifacts. Apparently large tracts of the Fertile Crescent were ruined by salinization and overgrazing before Roman times. Deforestation took a toll in China thousands of years ago. Within "high" civilizations vast numbers of peasants, including European peasants, remained illiterate and ordinarily remote from both politics and the cash economy.

On the whole, however, urbanism and settled agriculture resulted in fewer languages and fewer social patterns. Though ideologies changed incessantly, empires rose and fell, technology and procedural refinements multiplied, human identity was channeled into a few dozen styles of life (in the broad sense used by Toynbee and Spengler). More complexity but less diversity has been the trend, intensified in the last two hundred years by industrialism.

It is by no means clear whether this trend works for or against our species in the long run. Ultimately we may be specks in a cosmos beyond comprehension anyhow. Substituting complications of our own making for natural diversity may or may not be a viable use of our genetic endowment—acquired a million or more years before the first wheat was planted. But the narrowing at least facilitates self-awareness. We see that human collectivities have preserved only so many paths, that history has already herded us down one or another of these paths. By definition, traveling along one path forecloses options that belong to others. With regard to identity, however, we could do with more awareness of experiences available only *because* of following a definite path.

One of the main bifurcations of fate is sometimes expressed in terms of "Eastern civilization" versus "Western civilization." The geography of the terminology is shaky. Traditional Japan, for example, in some ways resembled feudal Europe more than it did China or India.

Conversely, it would be hard to find a more ruthless despotism than the Third Reich. The general drift of the terms is nevertheless understood.

An "Eastern" society is highly centralized—what Marx and Karl Wittfogel after him meant by despotic. In principle, lines of authority and status descend in a perfect pyramid from the Son of Heaven to the enslaved orphan of the lowest coolie. Power may under unfortunate circumstances turn out to be fractured, subverted, or misused but never *rightfully* divided. The ideal is monolithic. The word for a "Western" society is *pluralistic*. By fiat it may be, but autonomy is apportioned among institutions, blocs, and associations of many kinds —distributed as well as collected—on the (often vain) assumption that leeway for competitive jostling, spheres of influence, and degrees of home rule will satisfy urges that might otherwise lead to secession or lethal struggles for domination. Let-a-hundred-flowers-bloom is a daring and perhaps unworkable idea in the East. Conformity is a needlessly exaggerated bugaboo in the West.

Considering how fundamental pluralism is to Western identity, the rhetorical pallor of the word *pluralism* is surprising. Modern Western languages contain many expressions generated in the course of practicing pluralism. *Antithesis*, for example, harks back to the classical Greek habit of pairing opposites. The splitting of the chorus about 600 B.C. led to the creation of individual dramatic characters, whose "dialectic" was borrowed by the philosophers. The Romans perfected adversarial procedures at law and bequeathed related notions such as jurisdiction, render unto Caesar, et cetera, later extended in the role of devil's advocate and related aspects of ecclesiastical tribunals. The image of social estates—those who fight, those who pray, and those who work—guided medieval Europeans. Separation of powers, checks and balances, came out of the early modern period. First among peers, good fences make good neighbors, every tub on its own bottom, and similar bromides persisted in the nineteenth century. *Consensus* in recent political rhetoric, *market share* in business jargon, and the like continue to presuppose a pluralistic way of organizing social relations. Yet who would use *pluralism* in poems, creeds, eloquent dialogue? The word reeks of Govt. 202. Writers are likely to reach for "freedom" or "liberty" (although the latter is old-fashioned), but these bear many other connotations and in any case again have to do with practicing pluralism rather than conceptualizing it. Only William James, who discovered *pluralism* working as a humble technical term in disputes over formulating ultimate reality as a set of principles versus a single paramount principle, gave the word a star turn. He made it stand for the plenitude of being, his sense of the abundance and variety of encounters and meanings in the world, an allusion to the lushness and openness of existence suggested in a rustic way by the biblical metaphor "green pastures." But he had no successors in that respect.

The language from which a strong word ought to have come down to us is Akkadian, one of the two written languages of the Babylonians and the Assyrians (Sumerian being reserved by them for special literary uses). According to the archaeologist C. C. Lamberg-Karlovsky, the Akkadian words transliterated as *anduram* and *misharum* conveyed much the same meaning as *freedom* and *equality* do in the West now. Furthermore the noun *subarrum* appears to have been akin to the modern concept of a natural right to impartial application of the law. So unusual were such concepts in comparison with the world norm of absolutism that Lamberg-Karlovsky and others speak of a Near Eastern Breakout, signifying a unique cultural commitment to reciprocity, consensus, and division of power—in short, pluralism as a way of organizing society. In ancient Egypt, China, and Mesoamerica, by contrast, society was modeled on a layered universe. Pharaoh was thought of as a god, descended from gods and divinely sanctioned to promulgate whatever he pleased. In China, according to Chang Kwang-chih, a portion of the wealth extracted by the original ruling class was invested not in more weapons and more retainers but in securing a monopoly on communication and legitimacy. Early rulers took exclusive control of shamanistic religion, art, ritual, and ethical codes (particularly as they applied to social stratification) and imposed themselves as the sole link between heaven and earth. At the apex of Maya societies sat a supreme ruler—priest, commander, and lawgiver—and, according to Gordon Willey, "there is no evidence of any counter-balancing power within the chiefdom or state that could have held him in check." Against such patterns, the Mesopotamian assumption of moral, legal, institutional, and communal restraints on royal power indeed stands out.

But of course Akkadian was a dead language before the time of Jesus. Although loan words passed into Hebrew and conceivably Solon's reforms in Athens were based upon Mesopotamian models, Akkadian influences are almost impossible to detect in Greek and Latin. Any written exchanges between Mesopotamia and Mediterranean peoples may have been lost in the dawn of the classical age. Mesopotamian influence may have been filtered and refracted through the Hittites, Israelites, and Phoenicians. Possibly tribal inclinations toward pluralism were firmly in place all round the Mediterranean basin before the Sumerians built cities, and no further influence was necessary to sustain pluralism. In any case the Western elite who wrote in Latin and Greek down to the Industrial Revolution knew next to nothing of Mesopotamia. For them and still more or less for us it was rubble buried deep beneath Persia and Islam. Only since the nineteenth century has Akkadian become decipherable at all, and then only provisionally, in fragments, by a handful of scholars at the mercy of whatever tablets happened to survive.

Linguistic connections aside, moderns purport to be needy for roots, confused and anguished about their identity. If so, Mesopotamia is the culture for them to explore. There, on a large scale over a long stretch of time in complex forms, pluralism flourished. Many aspects of Mesopotamian life would seem natural to a proconsul, an abbot, a cabinet minister, a policymaker. In this pluralistic culture everything not perceived to be harmful was kept, but much that was new was added. If Edmund Burke or James Madison had written a romance of the ancient world, they might have reinvented their Mesopotamian predecessors. Mesopotamia was the locus classicus of Western ways.

The heart of Mesopotamia lay between the Tigris and Euphrates rivers. Most of present-day Iraq and Iran was included, a piece of Turkey, and a corridor west to the Mediterranean through what are now Lebanon and Syria. Sumerians, Babylonians, and Assyrians were the dominant groups, divided into rival city-states and kingdoms but generally independent of outsiders, interacting at various times with Palestinians, Elamites, Hittites, and other neighbors, vying with Egypt as the nearest superpower, and trading as far away as India. Invading Quti, Kassites, Hurrians, Amorites, and Arameans seized Mesopotamian cities on occasion; but apparently they were domesticated as readily as the Chinese domesticated invaders, for their presence is known mostly through an outcropping of foreign personal names. By about 2800 B.C. the Sumerians had assembled elements of civilization —cities, writing, governance at a distance. Around 2300 B.C. Sargon I broke free of the Sumerians and established a capital at Akkad, from which time through assimilation and extinction the Sumerians gradually disappeared as a separate people, although their written language was kept very much alive alongside Akkadian dialects till the end. In 538 B.C. the Persians under Cyrus II squelched for all time the political and cultural independence of Babylonia and with it any chance of resurgence for Assyria, interlocked with but destroyed as an empire by Babylonia in alliance with the Medes early in the previous century.

The chief rediscoverer was Henry Layard, an Englishman in the intrepid style who poked into a mound one day in the 1840s and found Nineveh. The magnificent winged bulls and other treasures that flowed into European museums caused great excitement. The Bible was still in the bones of Europeans, and Old Testament names such as Nebuchadnezzar, from what is now labeled the Chaldean dynasty, fired their imagination. Many Christians and Jews were happy to find the Bible "proven" as decipherment of Akkadian texts began (with the help of multilingual texts found in Persian ruins) and titillated by Babylon the sink of iniquity. Having endured this popular reaction, serious Assyriologists later had to temper enthusiasm for Mesopotamia the cradle of high technology, whose temples, dams, calendars, wagons, and the like were seen as precious forerunners to the wonders of steam and steel. As late as the 1960s the Assyriologist Leo Oppenheim was compelled to curb historians of science by pointing out that Akkadian plant lists were exercises in lexicography, not the genesis of botany.

It is true that in Realpolitik the Mesopotamians were as bad as great powers elsewhere, which is to say very bad indeed. They made conscious use of buffer states and forced resettlements of population. From the Assyrian frontier post of Mari, an official with manpower problems suggested to the king that "one of the guilty men in prison could be slain, and his head cut off and taken round the towns . . . , so that the troops may take fright and therefore assemble as quickly as possible." The original Sargon came up with such an overweening honorific for himself—King of the Four Quarters of the Earth—that his disheartened Sumerian competitors could think of nothing better than to copy it.

It is also true that Mesopotamians possessed both carnal and engineering know-how. The Assyrian ruler Esarhaddon put into a treaty an ingenious curse that would supposedly fall on the Medes if they broke it: "Let Venus, most brilliant of stars, cause your wives to lie in the bosom of your enemies before your very eyes." To reach a high standard of living was perhaps a greater achievement for the Mesopotamians than for the Egyptians. The Nile normally crests at the best time in the agricultural cycle, and it rises and falls slowly enough to do more good in depositing silt and replenishing the water table than harm in eroding fields and dikes. The Tigris and Euphrates by comparison tend to rise late, high, and abruptly, carry a great deal of coarse detritus, and rush away. By no means could an irrigation network be taken for granted once in place. Over fifteen hundred years after Sargon of Akkad, experiments in hydraulic engineering were still being tried, to result under the Assyrian king Sennacherib in the construction of the first aqueduct in the Mediterranean world. (Sennacherib also introduced, or took credit for introducing, the cotton plant into Assyria.) Furthermore, given the absence of currency, Mesopotamians were remarkably efficient at distributing commodities.

In evildoing, technology, and logistics, then, Mesopotamians held their own among early civilizations, but hardly more than that. Their particular distinction was to regard autonomy too as something that could be distributed.

The Mesopotamian way was to concede de facto corporate status to any plausible group that performed a function or actively possessed a resource acceptable to the community. Whatever their general social standing, virtually all *practitioners* (except slaves, of whom there were proportionately fewer toward the end of Mesopotamian civilization) were allowed a measure of control over their operations and a kind of custody over their occupational domain. Diviners and exorcists, for example, were middle-class professionals who compiled indices of dreams and omens and who were consulted by all classes, if anything more by the literate than by the ignorant. A solemn business theirs was, forecasting the gods' decisions as we now forecast Federal Reserve policy, and yet they were independent of the temple priests. If in Mesopotamia an activity grew appreciably in scope or complexity, new organizations and lines of work usually formed, each with its own measure of autonomy and separate identity much like the special disciplines that break off from older sciences today. Generally it was better cultural politics to let a new line of activity go its own way than to try to manage an expanding conglomerate. Other organizations would endorse separation in principle to justify their respective prerogatives and would gang up in practice to resist domination by any one rival organization.

The system benefited from a comparative lack of ideological rigidity. Over time the emphasis in warfare shifted from chariots to massed cavalry to loose formations to archers, and apparently no one had to ascend the mount for new commandments to make the changes. A related benefit was resilience of the parts, which were not fatally prone to be squeezed and drained from the center (as in imperial Rome) and which did not necessarily wither if the head were lopped off (as in the Spanish seizure of the Inca empire).

Friction of course was the cost of a pluralistic culture, energy spent in adjudication, haggling, keeping score. Items of food and drink placed in holy ceremony before the images of the gods were recorded by temple bookkeepers. There is something Seventh Avenue in the tone of surviving business correspondence. At a time when horses were scarce, one Ishi-Adad, a satellite chieftain of the Assyrian king, struck the characteristic note in a letter to Ishme-Dagan, son and main lieutenant of the overlord. "You indicated to me your wish to procure two horses, and I sent them to you," Ishi-Adad dictated to his scribe. "And now you have sent me twenty *minas* of tin! Have you not had your desire fulfilled by me and in full measure—and now you have sent me this scrap of tin!" Around 1350 B.C. a Babylonian king of the Kassite dynasty received a substantial present of gold from Egypt. Instead of thanking the pharaoh, he complained sharply of being short-weighted, relating in detail how he measured the metal, tried it in a furnace, and computed the amount of alloy with which the gold was mixed. "To each his own" might have been the motto of Mesopotamian architects. The typical structure was divided into chambers and courtyards that did not permit a view from one to the next. The sacred road that ran from a temple to the sanctuary where New Year ceremonies were held outside a city's gates joined the royal road from the palace in some cases and led to a different gate in other cases. Though these roads were broad and well maintained, the building fronts beside them sat raggedly at various distances from the edge. Lesser streets branched and looped irregularly, but the density of structures alongside probably obscured natural contours. Akkadian cities offered few vistas.

A summary account of major Mesopotamian institutions is virtually an introduction to competitive pluralism. Kings operated their own bureaucracy and economy—household government reminiscent of Tudor practices, say, and a hundred other Western regimes—employing a corps of counselors, entertainers, servants, overseers and engineers, fiduciaries and bookkeepers, craftsmen and processors, farmers, drivers, and laborers in that domain. A separate civil service of administrators, superintendents, and tax gatherers carried out royal policy in the kingdom as a whole, and through a professional army the king reserved most military and police matters for himself. Within home territory he dealt separately with city dwellers (many of whom commuted to work outside city walls) and with a relatively large population who lived permanently in villages and encampments over which the cities had no jurisdiction. Evasion and resistance to central government was the norm among these villagers and clansmen, with the cities discreetly throwing their support as expediency dictated. The more distant possessions of the king, like the far-flung dominions of Hapsburg emperors, were divided along similar lines but with a variety of local customs and arrangements that had to be accommodated too. When they held Babylon in subjugation, the Assyrian kings used a separate title in the southern regions to gratify local pride. On the borders lay occupied territories, client states, and independent allies and enemies—all potentially scheming to change their status.

Kings styled themselves slaves of the gods and wrangled with temple priests, who designated themselves the same way, as to who was the more important "slave." The temple in each city was regarded as the property of one god, but others were worshipped there too, and the god of the capital was more "universal," an invitation to palace and temple to maneuver for relocation and divine upward mobility. Temple and palace were similar in workshop products, administrative procedures, and rewards and recruitment. So important was the storage and redistribution function of the temple that what might be called managerial head priests shared power with theological head priests. By far the majority of workers in the service of a temple did secular jobs.

Kings had palaces in one or more cities and were normally represented in all cities of the realm. Each temple ministered to a city. Yet every city claimed separate status and made a distinction between inhabitants who "belonged" and inhabitants who, because they were employed by the king or the temple, were merely "stationed" in the city. Time and again when kings forced or induced migration, city leaders regardless of benefits or losses referred to those arriving or departing as "refugees." Within cities further boundaries were drawn around craft guilds, trade associations, and the like, and the farming outside the walls was carried out by multiple relatively large organizations. Strong kings sought to draw wealth and talent into a royal city, often founding new capitals which would be "theirs." Mostly they succeeded, thus wasting the work of previous generations as canals silted up and older buildings and fields deteriorated. Almost immediately in boomtowns created by royal initiative, however, political efforts to temper the king's demands would develop. When the Akkadian system was running full blast, powerful cities won tax exemptions and other privileges at the same time that kings were scheming to create "company towns." Conquest of principal cities was a necessary objective for both alien invaders and warring Mesopotamian states, but their defense was an unpredictable affair, possibly involving local troops, district troops (beholden to a governor), and royal "troops of the land," any given contingent of which might have a political agenda of its own.

Naturally pluralism prevailed in the symbolic realm too. Ideas, images, and values both reflected social practices and reinforced them. The mental universe was constructed of distinct entities with separate functions and status.

Possibly a Mesopotamian poet was thinking of cosmic division of labor rather than wickedness when he wrote:

> What is good in a man's sight is evil for a god.
> What is evil to a man's mind is good for his god.

An abundance of diviners and omen readers sought clues as to what the gods wanted or had decided, but reports to the gods, so to speak, were channeled through the priests. Divine authority itself was segmented, proceeding neither from an indivisible godhead nor from a clear hierarchy. Marduk, a major god over large parts of Mesopotamia, was credited with fashioning heaven and earth but not with originating the substance from which they were made. No less than eight intermediary spirits were required to connect an individual with divine forces. In principle he or she could end up lost, overlooked, unprovided for—like a traveler without ticket or passport, a soldier without rank or orders. Four of the eight might be termed protective spirits, although it is not clear whether they were thought of as genies who accompanied an individual or as faculties built into an individual. *Ilu* linked humans to divinity (a spiritual walkie-talkie); *lamassu* shaped personality; *sedu* conveyed sexual vitality; and *istaru* watched over individual fate. In addition everyone held a place in the eternal scheme of things through *usertu;* and *simtu* was the medium for supernatural decrees or actions dealt to an individual ad hoc. Finally, a demon capable of procuring good things (good from the human viewpoint) and a demon capable of inflicting bad things trailed each person.

Language and literature exhibited the same taste for multiple domains and functions. As mentioned earlier, two written languages flourished. Structurally, Sumerian stopped just where it was; in transition from logograms to phonograms, when Akkadian established itself as the more common language. The word list was frozen. Evidently Sumerian served some positive notion of linguistic conservation, for scribes mastered it generation after generation, meticulously reserved certain genres for it, and still at the time of the Persian conquest could re-create tropes from Ur with undiminished skill. Akkadian, which seems to have been the chosen medium for the opposite notion of linguistic change, underwent significant structural development up through the Old Babylonian period. Set structure and standardized formulas for wording and arrangement of content subsequently prevailed, but the Mesopotamians did not force the results of migrations, invasions, political upheavals, and innovations into a closed lexicon. Akkadian word lists lengthened, and variations of formulas were introduced. From the absence of biography, satire, adventure stories, and several other forms of literature, some modern scholars speculate that a whole separate body of writing on perishable material such as wood or leaves may have existed. Two kinds of writing material and two branches of scribes would be appropriate for Mesopotamia, and perhaps oral storytelling or recitation to boot, its practitioners separate from the scribes. It is known that the passion for competitive pluralism gave rise to a genre called the "disputation" in which various domestic animals, tools, and household objects were personified in a style that to modern ears sounds like rival agency heads making a pitch before a legislative committee. In one of these an ox says:

> From beginning to end of the year I find food;
> I have fodder in abundance and spring water in profusion.
> Change thy way of life and come away with me.

At which point a horse speaks up:

> Without me, the fiery steed,
> Nor king nor prince nor lord nor noble fares upon his way.
> The horse is like a god, stately of step;
> Whilst thou and the calves wear the cap of servitude.

Similar verbal contests were staged between summer and winter, the axe and the plow, and so forth.

Thus it went. Branching and twigging in the professions, of course. One category of medical practitioners diagnosed illness, and another prescribed treatment. Admixtures in art. Zigzags were a favorite decorative device—perfect for proceeding in several directions at once. The winged bulls and wild asses in palace art are stylized, unforgettably so, and yet ripple naturalistically with muscle and tendon.

Such a sample as has been given here of Mesopotamian institutions and forms leaves the impression of an extremely contentious culture, a muddled culture, and a wasteful culture. But all cultures are contentious, muddled, and wasteful to some degree, just as all are functional, ordered, and integrated to some degree. Configuration varies more than elements from one to the next. Intrigue and factionalism, better concealed ideologically but perhaps more murderous, abound in monolithic empires. It is always touch and go as to how much brainpower gets mobilized for astronomy and philosophy, say, and how much for designing an ingenious inner stairway so that a Maya chief can appear atop the great pyramid as though from the sky and never be seen panting and scrambling to get there.

What distinguished Mesopotamia and put it at the head of a distinct group of civilizations was pluralism. And what distinguishes pluralism from other cultural configurations is reciprocity as an accepted principle. Mesopotamian kings were not absolute monarchs. Theoretically they were subject to law themselves and bound to administer law equitably to others under threat of being dispossessed of their lands by the gods. In practice they were constrained by temple priests, city elders, and unruly rural clans. All down the social scale —frequently through written codes, charters, and contracts—rights were tied to obligations, the legitimacy of obligations depended on reciprocity, and this way of organizing social relations was justified by the assumption that competing for individual satisfaction *under these rules* benefited the community as a whole. That violations and malfunctions occurred may be taken for granted. A large part of daily life undoubtedly consisted of the few pushing the many around. So far as total goods and services were concerned, particular monolithic civilizations may have outproduced the Mesopotamians.

To what extent pluralism abets prosperity and freedom is in fact hard to say. It may offer an edge, but to claim an assured outcome is merely Western bluster or self-deception. What pluralism did engender in Mesopotamia compared with regimented cultures, easily stalled by one too many oscillations toward megalomania or stupidity at the top, was what might be called participatory culture. When floods struck, when a dynasty toppled, when competition temporarily overloaded the system, middling citizens (including a substantial number of women wage earners) did not need new instructions from the top to go forward with the way of life.

Greece and Rome are supplementary reading. The West begins in Mesopotamia.

Feudalism:
We Should Be So Lucky

I used to think that medieval people were the ones who based their daily decisions on the intricate instructions of shamans.—Ellen Goodman, *Boston Globe* columnist

Laborare est orare.—Motto of the Benedictines

Feudalism was unknown in the Middle Ages. Coined in the eighteenth century, shortly before the American and French Revolutions, the word has from the beginning reflected modern purposes.

One line of formidable social critics and visionaries running from Voltaire to Marx used it ideologically. They identified the aristocrats and prelates remaining in their day as the most reactionary element in the centralized states that had supplanted medieval government, an element whose overthrow, they believed, would begin the overthrow of the absolutist state. Therefore they discredited this element by attributing its origins to an egregiously ignorant, superstitious, unjust, impoverished, and sadistic way of life—a lower stage of human development. Advances that impressed these apostles of modernism in mathematics, chemistry, physics, and medicine, in philosophy, classical studies, and linguistics, as well as the proliferation of secular and cosmopolitan art, were deemed to occur heroically over the opposition of diehard remnants of the backward feudal mentality.

As the costs and drawbacks of industrial society became clearer, a completely different line of critics used *feudalism* to console themselves. They hated the ugly materialism and crowded loneliness of modern life, and so they decided to locate everything they missed in the Middle Ages. Here the German romantics, the British pre-Raphaelites, and America's Henry Adams come to mind. For them the feudal order was the perfect organic society, a marvel of continuity and *gemeinschaft*, whose members all knew where they stood in the world and in the cosmos and whose bad eggs were more than offset by the prevailing harmony of faithful service with *noblesse oblige*. Not only was this an age of the purest spiritual ardor (when contemplated centuries later from Liverpool), but its pageantry was breathtaking and the satisfaction it took in craftsmanship (so skilled, so genuine) profound.

For their part, popular storytellers, illustrators, and theatrical companies found a commercial use for the Middle Ages. The subgenre they created took twists and turns of its own that had more to do with the exigencies of modern entertainment than with medieval life. Often the Satanic dimension of the sorcerer disappeared, for instance, and he became a sort of magical ombudsman. Mythical creatures tripped onto the page—among them the damsel, a female who did not exist below the waist. Except for the misuse of antiquated pronouns, the evil Black Knight spoke like the villain in a showboat drama. Eventually millions took it for granted that Errol Flynn should look as though he showered every morning before venturing forth in Sherwood Forest as Robin Hood. Over the years feudalism as entertainment departed so far from any reality save its own conventions that comic geniuses such as Mark Twain and the Monty Python crew were inspired to burlesque Ye Olde Knightehood.

Ironically, all the while that *feudalism* was being tailored to suit various modern users who paid little attention to veracity or each other, the medievalists—that is, trained historians, philologists, theologians, and legal scholars specializing in the period—were providing ever better information and stimulating interpretations of the real thing. Henry Maine, Numis Fustel de Coulanges, and Henry Charles Lea may be mentioned as early masters of valuable scholarship that has been building for 150 years and is still going strong. Because of cumulative work, improved methods, and the ability to trace developments over many generations and compare events in widely separated parts of Europe, late-twentieth-century medievalists in some respects know more about feudal society than anyone who lived in the Middle Ages. No relevance is intended, however. Rather, this scholarship enacts a modern program. As long as it doesn't cost too much and as long as they don't have to understand it, people educated in the modern mode want all possible data bases to be covered by experts. Although they hope the knowledge they offer is true, the experts —in this case medievalists—fulfill the contract first of all by being good modern methodologists. They bend over backward to distinguish historiographical reconstruction, an analytic and retrospective project based upon techniques and concepts of their own time, literally inconceivable in the past, from the experience of those who lived feudalism.

In Third World countries is where confusion, anachronism, and pseudo-relevance run amok. *Feudalism* has long been a favorite word among modernizing politicians and professionals in that setting. They use it to tar with the brush of backwardness rivals, foreign exploiters of the plantation sort, and conditions of poverty. They use it to signal that they personally are up-to-date individuals who know what it is to form cadres, wear a watch, and discuss Hawk missiles. They use it to vent frustration. (Understandably. Egypt, to cite one example of what there is to be frustrated about, received $2.5 billion in outside aid in the twenty years following World War II and at the end of that period had the same per capita income as she had in 1913.)

Feudalism thrown around in this style means anything from the storekeeper trying to collect on his bill to all ascriptive social configurations. Feudalism is whatever grandfather did and whatever was done to him. Cosmetics are feudal if traditional, modern if not, while establishing a legal system in which central authority takes precedence (in the manner of the Plantagenets, incidentally) is progressive.

To wit. "Nations striving to advance with a medieval mentality are condemned to perish," proclaimed Ataturk in 1925. The Pan-African movement, a Ugandan official told an interviewer in the early 1960s, would not tolerate those who "insist on living in the feudal eighteenth century." "We are a feudal society," said a former member of India's parliament in 1989. "Our education system does not teach respect for women."

Such remarks are not inevitably nonsensical. The Brazilian *fazenda* was a prime example of an institution truly derived from feudalism that lasted well into the modern period. When nineteenth-century Brazilian authorities ascertained that a sufficient number of masterless people had settled a portion of the back country, title to the land would be given to one or another prominent oligarch. Thereupon the pioneers automatically became tenants on his fazenda and, whether or not also liable for payments, held their place on condition of service to him. Still, more often than not, the remarks are nonsensical. What until recently both Westerners and local modernizers called "feudalism from time immemorial" in many Muslim countries has been discovered to consist of practices, privileges, and upper-class families established about a century ago. It would be wondrously enlightening to resurrect a twelfth-century Anglo-Norman bishop and put him in the same chamber with Pramila Dandavate, the Indian legislator and feminist quoted above. He tempers her hopes for the historical worst by citing the *Rotuli de dominabus*, a survey showing that surviving female offspring under Henry II's wardship outnumbered surviving male offspring 155 to 138. She expounds the hypothesis that the world is round and contains India, then explains to him what a lesson plan is and what a public school is in her "feudal" society. Together in due course they work up a honey of a women's studies unit (or *fasciculus* as the bishop calls it).

As usual, Third World nations fell for the salesman's patter and received damaged goods, discontinued models, and poor directions. Properly speaking, feudalism and the terms associated with it refer to the social organization of Western Europe from the ninth century through the fifteenth century. For today's debt-ridden countries this strict definition is anything but academic. In that place and time happened to occur an outstanding instance of a people enriching themselves from a baseline of poverty and weakness. A case can be made for the Middle Ages as a series of strides toward abundance—less in the sense of living high, spreading wealth, or avoiding waste than in the sense of engendering a culture of productivity. Traditional Japan is the only other place where feudalism existed. Since alienable land was transferable there only among vassals of the same lord, since extreme emphasis was given to the obligations of inferiors as against reciprocal obligations of superiors, and since the samurai generally disdained technological change, purists would exclude it. Yet Japan's rapid transformation into a modern industrial power—the fitness and readiness of its culture for the transformation—is precisely what clinches its claim to a feudal past.

Modern affluence is an enlargement and outcome of the old order, not a break. Living up to the inheritance may be the problem in the long run. Has population growth raised the quality of modern life, as it did in feudal times? Has public finance been put on a more solid footing? Has trust been restored by replacing institutions that lose legitimacy?

The Dark Ages that followed Roman collapse in the West deserved their name. Decaying towns, subsistence farms and hamlets, roving tribal bands barely out of the Stone Age scratched a poor living among vast tracts of unused land. Raiders, invaders, and local strongmen went after everything worth pillaging as fast as it germinated. As C. Warren Hollister has noted, utter economic ignorance was the rule. "Merovingian government does not seem ever to have risen above the predatory level. To the typical Merovingian king, the state was simply a source of income and power which he exploited as a leech exploits its host. Indeed, in their promiscuous alienations the Merovingians demonstrated their incapacity even as predators."

But Third World countries do not need remote lessons on poverty and violence. The more instructive point is the way economic activity was incorporated into the feudal order that pulled Europe out of a pit. The Romans had a gift for organization, transport, bringing mass labor to bear on public works, quickly converting wealth into visible opulence that served as a kind of vicarious public good. However, an inordinate amount of talent and ambition was drawn into deficit activities—administration, war, and consumption. Overhead tended constantly to outstrip production. (It has been estimated that at the height of Roman order nineteen people living on the land were required to support one city dweller.) Leaders were unfamiliar with primary work, and in a pinch they were more likely to put the squeeze on existing resources than to expand the productive base. When the supply of fresh slaves dwindled, fields were abandoned, and labor shortages developed in the towns, the Romans responded, as administrators will, with decrees. A doubly anomalous category was created—the *colonus,* an outsider settled on another's land and a free person who could not leave without permission. In some Roman territories toward the end, sons were frozen into their fathers' occupations by law. By contrast the medieval order made greater use of trade-offs. In some places a son gained the right to inherit his father's property if he demonstrated that he had learned his father's trade. A large number of peasant cultivators acquired permanent tenure by clearing and improving land—an early example of what became known in the West as "sweat equity." According to a ninth-century ordinance that has been quoted by David Herlihy, entrepreneurship was protected even before slavery was abolished: "It is not allowed for a man to take from his slave the *pecunia* he has acquired with his own labor." Clearly one of the things feudalism means is a relative shift from coercion toward incentives.

Perhaps the greatest incentive devised in the medieval system was to link intimacy, coresidence, and procreation with production. A man was expected to have property or an occupation before marrying. A woman was expected to marry outside the circle from which she might inherit and to bring capital with her into the new household. Marriage was the most standardized institution in feudal society, virtually the same as a moral and legal unit from top to bottom of the social hierarchy. The family farm and the family workshop were the most common enterprises, and beyond what they owed to the demesne of the lord in customary labor services and rents, most families worked for themselves and could pass on assets to heirs. Kings much preferred fiefs (held by the tenant or vassal as an individual and only as long as he provided the required services) over allods (permanent, unconditional, heritable title to land). In England after 1066, for example, all land was conceived to owe service to the king. Lords held theirs as tenants-in-chief of the monarch; rear vassals and knights held theirs from lords. Throughout Europe, however, especially after 1300, fiefs tended to become heritable and partible and thus more distinctly family property. This departed sharply from the Roman model. Given the large number of slaves and unmarried workers of various status in barracks and tenements and given differences in legal standing and custom from class to class, the "household" was too incommensurate an arrangement to be used by Roman census takers. In late antiquity large numbers of middle- and low-ranking women and their families of origin saw little advantage in marriage over a single woman supporting herself. Already by the late republican period a number of Romans conceived of economic resources as in effect a pie of fixed size from which too many people were nibbling.

In the medieval context, by its insistence on monogamous marriage and its prohibition against marriage between close relatives the church checked accumulations of women and wealth in a few powerful households. Pope Alexander III's decree in the twelfth century that the spoken consent of eligible partners alone rendered a marriage valid also had far-reaching "antitrust" results, a subject on which David Herlihy's insights are worth quoting at length:

> This principle had extraordinary consequences. The Church, in effect, affirmed that no one and no institution could interfere with the right of a man and a woman, otherwise eligible, to marry or not to marry. The manorial or feudal lord lost control over the marriages of his serfs or vassals. The doctrine even limited the authority of the Church. . . . Failure to obtain the nuptial blessing, to endow the bride, or to publish the banns of marriage (after this was required by the Fourth Lateran Council in 1215) were prohibitive impediments; they rendered the marriage illicit but not invalid. The offending couple were liable to reprimand and penances but their marriage stood.
>
> Perhaps most decisively, the principle undermined the authority of the parents, fathers in particular, who might seek to arrange or prevent the marriages of their offspring. The father . . . was helpless in the face of an elopement. The Church's doctrine was a damaging blow to paternal authority and by itself assured that the medieval family could never develop into a true patriarchy.

That the pure doctrine of consent was frequently violated in practice through threats and bullying, emotional blackmail, property manipulation, and outright violence may be assumed. Since the family was constituted as in part an economic institution in the first place, ways were found, especially by the well-to-do, to tie business considerations to honorable consent. Among noble French families in the twelfth century, for example, younger sons were taught that they should win a prize in war or the hand of an heiress if they wanted to marry. Many accepted an ecclesiastical career. After 1300 noble families throughout Europe kept large landholdings intact through primogeniture (creating senior and cadet branches of the family) and entailment (enjoining heirs from selling or otherwise alienating an estate). Managing land on an efficient scale was deemed productive; a landless aristocrat with cash (even if he were one's own child) was thought to be a parasite. Italian families who drew their wealth from banking, trading, or various urban professions and services instead of farmland formed *consorteria:* corporations to manage in the collective interest the revolving funds, flowing inventories, urban facilities, and intangible assets associated with such enterprises. Thus the house of Bardi in Florence, which numbered sixty households related by blood in 1427, took care in notarized contracts to reckon ownership in numerical shares and to install specific officers in charge of the business.

Institutions beyond the family were likewise "economized" regardless of their various functions. An explicit and more or less monitored source of support was a constituent part of social identity. This was obvious in the name *mendicant order*. It was masked in the name *contemplative order*, and yet at the great abbeys more than anywhere appeared the society's full range of agriculture, animal husbandry, and food processing, building and sanitation techniques, handicrafts and furnishings, toolmaking, bookkeeping. A gift of serfs ("manpower") from pious laymen to these humming enterprises was often valued over inert treasure. If an individual's source of support proved unusually fruitful, that in itself might alter social identity. Suppose a miller's competitors were wiped out by a flood and his trade doubled or tripled. Or say a prosperous peasant cleared new fields and reaped a profit repeatedly before his landlord realized what had occurred. Whatever the source, if a Christian acquired property equal to the *feudum militis* (knight's fee), he was both entitled and obligated to serve as a knight. Correspondingly, a knight too poor to serve ran a risk of losing status. Although class solidarity and mercenary soldiering retarded the fall of impoverished gentlemen, possessions as well as blood were important.

Not only an identifiable source of support but also a contribution to social overhead went with every principal function. Nobles had a great deal more to do than cultivate martial skills, collect tribute, and bear attendance on their overlords. (By the thirteenth century formal attendance on the average took only about a fortnight per year.) Every noble of consequence managed a household, an estate, and a bureaucracy as well as a military contingent. He administered law and regulated markets in his domain, activities sometimes more complicated and time-consuming than laying siege. Peter of Dreux, duke of Brittany, for example, who coveted land granted to André de Vitré by King Philip Augustus, founded a market at Saint Aubin in order to ruin business at a fair licensed by André nearby. When settlement was reached in 1237, a clause in the agreement imposed a change of date for market day at Saint Aubin. As more and more tenements became patrimonies toward the beginning of the fourteenth century, heirs continued to pay "relief" to a lord upon investiture because, among other reasons, they were being allowed to command resources relevant to the common weal (much as utility companies hold a franchise from government in modern mixed economies). By the same token, master craftsmen were by no means free to tend to private business only—fabricating articles and supplying customers. Through the guilds they were involved in training and certification for the good of the trade, collective bargaining, and local government. Besides having more to do than "their job," a number of people seemingly sought more to do. The category of the liege lord preserved the feudal ideal of undivided loyalty while allowing the gentility to subcontract their services to other patrons according to demand. Some laborers likewise reconciled propriety with economic opportunity by farming one estate while acknowledging bondage to another. From such attitudes and behavior at times resulted economic ratios impressive by modern standards. In Anglo-Norman England about two hundred lords and fifty-five hundred rear vassals and knights managed a population of approximately one million. Though the clergy might simplify their role in slogans such as "serving Christ" and "caring for souls," the medieval church resembled a gigantic network of holding companies, subsidiary corporations, branch plants, research laboratories, welfare agencies, and political action committees. Monasteries, universities, military orders, cathedral chapters, holy offices, sees, and parishes pursued separate sources of income, kept separate books, recruited "personnel" separately, operated by separate charters, bylaws, and canons. Collectively of course they performed the bulk of Europe's clerical work in the modern sense as well as their own. Although much has been made of the church's condemnation of usury—an attitude variously viewed in modern times as an ignorant medieval economic impediment and as an aspect of Christian piety—it may have been wise to make direct investment in production as attractive as purely pecuniary activity to those with liquid capital. In any case, it is not surprising with regard to multinational church enterprise that simony was the hotter issue at the time.

Also built into medieval social identity was another economic preoccupation: What use of resources does a given role sanction? Modern accounting, chockablock with categories such as "allowable business expense," "shadow rate of return," and so forth has greatly refined this mode of thought but certainly did not invent it. In the crisis provoked by the Franciscans over the issue of whether servants of Christ ought to possess wealth, the church reflected and appealed to a worldview that produced the concept of fiduciary. The church, it was argued, managed the patrimony of the saints and paid spiritual dividends to the faithful. In principle no one in orders or in ecclesiastical office was personally entitled to more than a simple living, but to acquire, husband, display, and expend wealth for the propagation of the faith was a sacred responsibility.

Another characteristic of medieval culture that invites the label "proto-business civilization" was a disposition to make relationships contractual. Oaths of fealty stressed transaction (*facere*) over bestowal (*dare*), and contractual obligations took precedence over kinship ties. Under Alfred the Great, for example, it was unlawful to bear arms against one's lord in defense of a kinsman. The twelfth-century Italian *Book of Fiefs* prescribed that a vassal must aid his lord against everyone, including the vassal's own father, sons, and brothers. Reciprocity —implicit in contractual relationships and a check on a purely autocratic "mandate from Heaven"—was provided for. Carolingian law permitted unilateral cancellation of vassalage if the vassal were assaulted by the lord, who had supposedly undertaken to protect him. Later, faithless lords were classified as felons, while fiefs held by faithless vassals automatically reverted. Because it included reciprocity, fealty could evolve into a legitimate object of trade. A similar turn of mind was evident among commoners in the steady conversion of service into fixed payments in money and kind. The corollary idea that nonperformance often called for economic remedy alongside moral and criminal sanctions also emerged: alternative means for carrying out the intended function; redeployment of resources to another activity. On that assumption lords sometimes repossessed fiefs from childless vassals. Women held fiefs in the later Middle Ages, but on the understanding that a husband or sworn substitute would deliver the military service due. Even among quite unequal parties some due process was interposed. Important rights might be denied to weak fief-holders, such as legal jurisdiction of any sort, but the denial itself would be spelled out in a charter. Royal courts stipulated that lords were bound by guidelines devised in their own courts, and in certain cases a serf's duties were fixed by the custom of the manor rather than a current master's pleasure. Insofar as practice approximated principle, feudal society aimed at an environment of predictability, presumably more cherished by business executives than knights-errant. It is not surprising that some of the best brains in Europe did battle on the field of legalistic trickery. Chertsey Abbey in England, for instance, in 1285 forged and foisted on Edward I a charter that prohibited royal officers from entering the abbey's lands.

Appropriately, feudal society made a strong showing in the technology of basic production. Between 900 and 1400 appeared the cam, the power bellows, the waterpower sawmill, the mechanical clock, the magnifying lens, the heavy plow, and the horse collar. The novelty of modern factories and assembly lines has been overestimated in general. A similar instrumental rationality shaped Chinese waterworks, the Inca messenger service, the food-distribution systems of Assyrian temples, and who knows how many other ancient facilities. It is specifically unwarranted to draw an impassable line between modern and feudal society in this respect. A medieval stoneyard such as the one at Orvieto—with its equivalent of director, superintendent, comptroller, design department, foremen, specialists (who might, for example, do only hair and hands on statuary), and less skilled workers doing repeatable tasks broken into short segments—resembled a Detroit production plant.

In the tricky matter of joining authority and operational responsibility, it may be more accurate to speak of deterioration in modern times instead of enlargement and continuity. Sharp differences in pay and privilege between those who run an organization and those who do its work are not especially modern or medieval or even Western. They can be found anywhere. However, modern organizations breed policymakers who literally do not know how their directives will be carried out and functionaries who do not know the purpose of their tasks. Hence an extravagant number of "coordinators" to try to hold things together. In the medieval system, better attuned to production, authority and operational responsibility tended to converge. Understanding the work was a qualification for managing. Performing a task conferred authority. In eleventh-century and twelfth-century Poitou, for example, there were holders of allodial land, landholders who were vassals of the king, and landholders who were vassals of the count. In theory justice should have been dispensed to these groups by different authorities, but that was impractical, and so the count was designated to enforce public order for all. This line of counts had no particular clout. No one pretended the arrangement was procedurally consistent. The counts were picked because they were on the spot—authority assigned functionally—and because then the work would get done. A related boon to medieval productivity was the widespread capacity to replicate the whole culture, material and symbolic. Each sizable port or ecclesiastical center or estate could if necessary perform the entire repertoire. And that repertoire included, whatever one's occupation, factoring economics (not identical with personal gain) into one's sense of the world. The Spanish captains, the finest soldiers in Europe at the end of the Middle Ages, are often characterized as men obsessed with empty honors, destructive and vain, prone to throw money away on trappings and revels, men who would rather die than do anything useful. Yet from these captains came the saying "He who wins is the one with the last *escudo*"—meaning that to pay and provision the troops counts ahead of prowess and strategy.

Mobility is important to civilizations with a strong sense of economics—capacity and will to shift factors of production relatively fast, to retire and start up, move with the market. Money, materials, people, information, and organizations must circulate and recombine. One of the first signs of this way of doing things in the early Middle Ages was a general movement of the population away from a free status into a servile status, which under prevailing conditions offered more security and a better livelihood. Once feudal institutions were firmly rooted and population had grown, a wave of clearing new land followed and quarrying, mining, woodcutting, and more intensive hunting and fishing on the still considerable wild tracts. Here the incentives touched upon above came into play: tenure, or at least a share of the gains for effort. After 1000 the stick replaced the carrot for three centuries or so. Further population pressure stimulated a search for further resources with or without equitable rewards. During the same interval, when their income from pillage and tribute declined, many of the great families consciously looked to more intense cultivation of their estates as a basis for higher rents. From the Black Death, the Hundred Years War, and a consequent radical decline in population between the early fourteenth century and the early fifteenth century, which many contemporaries feared was permanent, followed another flexible response. More power machinery was installed, specie was used in a more sophisticated way, more freedom was allowed to commercial centers, and more traffic flowed over lengthened transport lines. Per capita income rose between 1320 and 1480, not merely as an arithmetical result of population decrease but also because capital, machinery, and reorganization were used profitably. Compared with traditions in India and China, say, where the distinction between individual and family was faint, a taste for circulation was present in medieval Europe. In many regions young people before marriage circulated among households as servants and laborers. Scholars moved from school to school. Merchants searched for new markets (this was the period of great land voyages). Artists jumped from patron to patron. The church, although a diversified, multitudinous operation, much given to policy revisions and reassignments, obstructed the main current of Western culture by monopolizing the interpretation of experience. Thus the Reformation can be viewed as the bursting of a bottleneck, the result of impeding mobility and circulation.

A scan of centuries of history over a large area is bound to turn up traces of nearly everything human, freakish extremes as well as bits of the universal. To demonstrate a few instances of economic adeptness in the medieval record is nothing. Rather, the contention here is that feudalism was an economic success on a large scale because of values that mattered and operated in the common life of the time and place.

Economic adeptness, however, is no one-and-only "key" to understanding the Middle Ages. To place it in the foreground is worthwhile because it has so often been overlooked or ruled out in modern accounts, which present barons and abbots and their underlings as lumpish. Naturally the process of bringing economics forward pushes other traits such as ferocity and credulity into the background.

What can be said about feudalism to today's poor countries? If they want to modernize, they would probably do well to medievalize in the sense of spreading incentives, contractual relationships, operational responsibility, and mobility everywhere. To think of literally imitating a way of life, however, as it emerged from a historical marinade long gone, is idle. As to dissolving a way of life to make room for a new one of any kind, even the star utopians fudge that problem. "Wither away," "Enter the Kingdom of Heaven," they say lamely. It is easier to imagine a scholastic Idi Amin training up a harebrained corps of medievalists to provide ideological guidance than to imagine a truck driver in China dropping his assumption of despotism as the natural principle of public order.

With a great deal more certainty a moral for modern Westerners can be drawn from feudalism. If they actually made use of the knowledge they pay medievalists to compile, they would stop flattering themselves in an adolescent way that they are a brand new breed. The Commercial Revolution of the sixteenth century and the Industrial

Revolution of the late eighteenth century and early nineteenth century were built upon a medieval inheritance. Numerous direct carryovers in language, law, and education still govern what they say, how they deal, and what they learn. A ceremonial style endures, evident at weddings, parades, party congresses, popular rallies. Old distinctions between rank and skill persist, as in the role of "handlers" for American political candidates. Western culture of the past thousand years is very much of a piece.

Much of the agonizing of modern cultural critics has an adolescent flavor too, resembling the belief of every generation as it comes along that its garb and patter are the most sophisticated in the history of the world, its sexuality the most acute, its anxieties the least understood. The notorious modern theme of "rootlessness" has less to do with facts of historical continuity or discontinuity than with the vanity and convenience of thinking one owes nothing to the past. Likewise with "future shock," about which much alarm is expressed. The severity of the affliction is doubtful when it leaves the victims with the equanimity to make a full-scale analysis and critique, carry on an informal public forum, and yet support institutions and values that virtually guarantee further shocks. But then selective indifference to tradition has long been a Western trait. Many people took it calmly when they found one morning that they had become subjects of a king instead of a pope (Roger II in Sicily) or of an emperor unfamiliar with their country (Charles V in Spain). They took it in stride when God changed his mind rather abruptly about whether priests should marry.

The truth is that the economic bent of Westerners foments change but that they lack a cultural design for changes brought about by science. To a modest extent scientific activity existed in feudal society. Roger Bacon helped to lay the foundations for experiment when he observed that a cause which when repeatedly introduced results repeatedly in the same effect makes prediction possible. "Another consequence," wrote William of Occam, "is that every cause properly so-called is an immediate cause; for that cause which can be removed or posited without having any influence on the effect, and which when posited in other circumstances does not produce the effect, cannot be considered a cause." About 1300 Theodoric of Freiburg discovered by manipulating spheres and water that light is not linear. By that time most extant Greek writings on science had been translated. Optics, magnetism, and mechanics were deemed fit subjects for study as "natural magic." That we inherited some rudiments of science is only to be expected. *Nil posse creari de nilo.* What should alarm moderns is that we also inherited a meager cultural provision for science and have not advanced beyond it. Science itself has reached a level of magnitude beyond the medieval imagination. Collectively scientists have showed themselves amenable to any purpose whatsoever, from eliminating smallpox to blowing up the world. Meanwhile, however, we operate on the medieval assumption that science will not alter values. There is less consensus now than in 1300 on the accountability of scientists or on the value of idle curiosity.

The medieval legend of Faust was an uncanny expression of cultural premonition. Someone foresaw which strand in the scheme of values might break loose and, if so, force a change of Western identity. They may have feared this and through Faust tried to discourage it. Or they may have welcomed it and slipped a Promethean hero past the censors by bringing him to a bad end. It is impossible to say. But they knew exactly who they were and thus more or less who we are —so far.

Heresy

Imagine that in an empire long since broken up the ruler's birthday served as a deadline for settling or renewing debts. It would not be surprising if two hundred years later in a successor society with a different way of scheduling debts the banks closed each June 30 for something called Emperor's Day. Go to a town where the trains stopped running in 1942. Somebody there still lives on the wrong side of the tracks. When practices, ideas, institutions, and objects in everyday use change or disappear, words get stranded.

The fate of some words is analogous to the fall of a celebrity into obscurity. After a while people no longer know what the celebrity was famous for.

The fate of other words, if they are "preserved" in figures of speech, may resemble that of Stephen Crane's Maggie, a girl of the streets. A relatively clear meaning connected to a relatively intact social or mental setting made a phrase attractive initially. Once it becomes available rhetorically, however, writers and speechmakers use it as they please. Through repetition a formerly enticing expression descends into triteness and then into ordinary language where it is not even perceived as a figure of speech. Finally comes the degradation of mere syntactical survival.

Does it matter? Probably. People are happier with meaning than without. Truth is too difficult a project to muck up with filler language, vacated language. Events or relationships important enough to enter language raise issues that may come up again in human affairs.

Revolutionary is a good example of a word on the verge of becoming filler language. Though still strong in some contexts, it is eroding into a term with which to advertise office machines. Already in such a fashion the word *heresy* has drifted into limbo.

Heresy used to be as familiar and tangible as taxation. On the eve of modern times the church had the power to seize and punish dissenters (or the option of directing secular authorities to do so). A few grandfathers ago people killed each other over the proper age for baptism. Precious administrative resources were allotted to ensuring conformity at outposts remote from the supreme councils. Powerful opponents paid each other a backhanded compliment with the honorific "heresiarch." Doctrine and liturgy figured intimately in everyday life. It was clear even to the illiterate that struggles over salvation and damnation were high drama. Thus as modern societies took shape the use of heresy as a metaphor served well to underline conflicts in worldview and doctrine of many sorts. Those who praised empirical investigation over sacred texts and who advocated a purely civil order were recognizable under the old terms that they opposed. As more figurative liberties were taken with the word under new conditions, institutions, and ideologies, however, meaning drained out of it. In time it came into jocular use. "He committed heresy by showing up for the ceremony in jeans." Sloppy writers use it to point vaguely in the direction of disagreements that they have no intention of exerting themselves to understand. Say twenty economists attend an international conference and four or five of them favor revising assumptions about the importance of fluctuations in commodity prices. Journalists call this "heresy." A tennis coach believes fewer tournaments should be crowded into the year's schedule; the board that governs tournaments votes otherwise; the coach is said by his friends to be treated as a "heretic." At the same time, those who bear responsibility for the residual reality of the word—which is still on the church's books—and who know something about its history are flustered, unable to deal with the elementary distinction between an armed power and an unarmed power.

What was as comprehensible as taxation has become a nebulous marker, evident in the case of Hans Küng. In December 1979 Küng was censured by the Sacred Congregation for the Doctrine of the Faith. For challenging the dogma of papal infallibility and for questioning the divinity of Christ he was divested of the right to speak in the name of the church and as a consequence was removed from the post of Catholic theologian at the University of Tübingen.

Although this would have amounted to a Socinian heresy for sure four hundred years earlier, politic clergymen strained for language severed from history. Almost as though they dreaded a revival of invective from the age of zeal (heretic dog, devil's spawn, Beast of Rome, and the like), liberals gingerly replaced the *h* word with "limits to orthodoxy." Avery Dulles, S.J., less liberal, chose to sidestep sinister connotations by reducing history to a straightforward manual of procedures that need concern only a few church officials in an administrative capacity. "Popes and bishops should have the primary responsibility for determining questions of orthodoxy and heresy," he commented. "This option is in accordance with the traditional Catholic understanding of the pastoral office."

Sensing an opportunity to evoke lurid scenes of sadistic inquisitors and mauled victims, journalists went to the other extreme. *U.S. News and World Report* tried to sketch an old-time melodrama. Although unidentified ecclesiastics were said to "insist that the pontiff had not ordered any sweeping inquisition," unnamed liberal churchmen were alleged to warn of "new Vatican pressure" and to compare it to "the inquisitions of the 13th century." Yet the effect was ruined by the fact that Küng was not at that time excommunicated or even prevented from teaching theology as an individual.

The desire of churchmen to damp down conflict was probably more salutary than the urge of journalists to produce hot copy. However, tiptoeing around history or grabbing for a few potted historical allusions did not clarify the situation or refresh anyone's understanding of heresy. Yes, the Albigensian Crusade took place in the thirteenth century, Gregory IX established a papal inquisition outside the jurisdiction of bishops, and the Council of Tarragona called for harsher penalties against heretics. Yet the thirteenth century is also memorable for the founding of the Franciscans and the Dominicans— originally enjoined to espouse humility and charity—and for the protection of Aquinas by the papacy against local church officials. Some historians argue (though not in the spirit of Avery Dulles) that the significance of the thirteenth century was administrative: increased efficiency and the appointment of more scrupulous bishops allowed the church to calibrate its reaction to heresy as it had wanted to all the time. As to how it all came out, the explanatory power of conciliatory versus punitive is limited anyway. In the 1530s the Sacred College was dominated by *spirituali*, clerics who believed, contrary to Aquinas, that all persons could ultimately be saved by a merciful God and that Protestants could be reclaimed through Catholic self-reform. In the next generation such clerics were supplanted by zealots, and Pius V, a bookburner, became pope. The point is that neither group gained ground against the forces of modernity.

Since we are now well past the point where the forces of modernity can simply be equated with enlightenment, this is as good a time as any to review the concept of heresy. Problems of authority and assent are unavoidable in the business of being human. Setting up a framework of orthodoxy and heresy is one kind of management. What does it offer?

In reviewing heresy as it was conceived when Western societies regarded themselves bound together at the most fundamental level by religion, it is necessary to take ideas seriously. The modern assumption that conscious motives are nothing but a mask for "real" psychological, social, or economic causes gets in the way. This assumption reflects a post-Enlightenment culture that does not rate reason highly and is not good at reasoning. (Instrumental rationality is another matter, a heightening of animal intelligence.) If I tell you that all conscious explanations are a mask, either my explanation ipso facto conceals the truth or it is untrue. Although of course not devoid of fantasy, hypocrisy, and ritual, Christendom more than most religious configurations linked action to logic. If what Donatist heretics said were true, for example, sacraments administered by unworthy priests would have no validity, and the faithful put their souls in peril by going to church. If what Donatists said were not true, going to church would be insufficient, for failure to oppose their error might draw God's wrath. Hussites, to give another example of action (in this case political and military action) based on conclusions, all reasoned that the church erred. Yet the moderate Hussites (Utraquists), holding that the radical Hussites (Taborites) departed even farther from the truth than Rome on the doctrine of perfection, chose to fight on the side of the church.

A pure history of ideas has obvious limitations. Impatient with texts alone—disquisitions, missives, court documents—and faithful to the mentality of their own times, modern historians have calculated such factors as birth rates and distribution of land to uncover social reality. Thanks to them, the fact has been brought out that weavers, numerically overrepresented in heretical movements, were among the earliest wage workers. Besides such groups with a special relation to the economy, towns and universities (partly independent through charters) and mendicant orders (outside monasteries and parish postings) were focal points of heresy. There is reason to agree with the historian Jeffrey Russell that the higher clergy were the most conservative members of the feudal nobility.

To ideas and social class must be added obedience as an absolute value—beyond reason, beyond rank—for a rounded account of heresy. No one has developed this theme better than Edward Peters, who in *Heresy and Authority in Medieval Europe* concludes: "The variety of dissenting opinions and the specific contents of heretical beliefs matter less than the fact that they *were* heresies." Roughly speaking, a third of the picture of heresy is missing when the issue of obedience is left out. Indeed, more than a third of MS 894 in the University Library of Leipzig, listing scriptural passages suitable for the refutation of heretical tenets, defends practices of the church rather than articles of faith. Saint Bernard in a well-known sermon (ca. 1144) labeled lack of deference to clerics a Christian crime. He attacked heretics for "boldly usurping for yourselves the prerogative of those whose sanctity you have not." Bernard, who himself lived on bread, water, and boiled vegetables, fumed at a group of heretics for daring to abstain from cheese and milk. A late-thirteenth-century bishop in this tradition condemned certain pious women because they "refused obedience to men under the pretext that God was best served in freedom." Valdès, the twelfth-century merchant of Lyon blamed for the Waldensian heresy, came to grief not by giving his wealth away and not by denouncing clerical immorality but by preaching. The issue of who might bear witness incited later and more radical Waldensians to proclaim a universal priesthood of all believers (including women, though Valdès had sent his daughters to a convent when he was "born again"). "Until his insistent evangelism overrode the papal and archepiscopal prohibitions on preaching," observe W. L. Wakefield and A. P. Evans in *Heresies of the High Middle Ages*, "Waldes appears in every respect as a forerunner of Francis of Assisi; willingness to obey authority was the fundamental difference between them."

To accept the church's guidance on religion alone was not necessarily a defense. Around the year 1000 a French eccentric named Leutard, who had no objections whatsoever to doctrine, was classified as a heretic because he expressed outrage over clerics who did not live up to church standards (and possibly because he drew an audience). In 1077 one Ramihrd was burned to death by irate priests because while professing orthodoxy before a bishop he criticized the morals of the local clergy. On theological grounds the inquisition into the creed of Hans Böhm of Niklashausen around 1475 might have gone either way, but his execution was assured when he said that it would be easier to make a Christian out of a Jew than out of a priest. Not only was it wrong to disobey ecclesiastical authority, but it was wrong to seek justification for obeying. When a group of heretics at Cologne in the twelfth century promised to submit to the church if their leaders were rebutted in debate, they were "urged for three days to come to their senses" and then burnt.

Conversely, merely to espouse unorthodox ideas without flouting ecclesiastical authority subjected one to a moderate risk only. Although John Scotus Eriugena formulated peculiar doctrines—for example, that Eve was not a woman but an allegory for the senses—he escaped condemnation in his lifetime because he "never resisted the will of the universal Church." Amaury, a neo-Platonist logician and theologian at the University of Paris about 1200, was disgraced professionally and scolded by the pope for his ideas. Nevertheless, because he expressed his ideas politely and abstractly he died a free man of natural causes. So-called Amaurians who took up these ideas militantly and put themselves into competition with the orthodox clergy were imprisoned for life or burnt.

As a rule neither piety nor repentance could excuse failure to honor clerical authority, and sometimes the gravity of a heretic's sin depended less on offense given to God than on the church's public relations strategy. Thus Marbod of Rennes thought the capital crime of a certain evangelical preacher was to "cheapen the Church in the eyes of the common people." According to Roger of Hoveden in 1165, public displays of clerical supremacy took priority over quiet reclamation of heretical souls. "It is the duty of the prelates," he said, "to correct and punish their disobedience in front of everybody."

A particularly sordid episode of keeping up appearances occurred in the case of Jan Hus at the beginning of the fifteenth century. Hus —a doctor of theology, influential at court, rector of the University of Prague—came before the Ecumenical Council of Constance with a promise of safe conduct and eloquently put the proposition that since Christ was the true head of the church, then the papacy was a human institution and therefore an unworthy pope ought to be deposed. The reverend members of the council worked out a compromise. For simony, murder, sodomy, and fornication they removed the original John XXIII, disguising their act by expunging his name from the roll of popes. Hus they sent to the stake.

Many cases, many twists and turns. To make sense of heresy in Christendom it pays to hang onto the theme of spiritual monopoly. Disestablishment and secularization have disarmed churches. Yet even so, even today, at least for those who desire to remain communicants, there are echoes of a ferocious insistence on what lawyers would call the sole and exclusive right to define, dispense, and regulate religion.

Likewise to place heresy in a world context, religious or not, this same desire for monopoly ought to be kept in mind. Virtually all societies organize religious urges into fairly definite and to some degree compulsory beliefs and observances. Nearly always someone controls, leads, intercedes, addresses, or somehow delves into religion more intensely than the community at large. Inevitably, who they are and what they do intertwine with the overall distribution of power and resources. Usually over time alternative visions arise, social composition shifts, internal competition and external encroachments occur. It means very little, therefore, to inject the term *heresy* at just any point where conflict or repression surfaces. The word illuminates some situations and not others. In Islam, for example, heresy does not exist. In the words of the scholar Bernard Lewis: ". . . Since Islam has no councils or churches or hierarchy, there is no officially defined orthodoxy and there cannot therefore be any officially defined and condemned deviation from orthodoxy." Moreover, virtually all societies legitimate (one might say perfect) some pattern of domination. *Heresy* is a poor word to cover the case of a soldier punished for failure to salute, a worker fired for mocking the boss, an editor jailed for advocating honest elections, a wife beaten for disrespect to her husband. Heresy is not intrinsic to every variety of coercion or religion.

In searching for the boundaries of heresy outside its strict ecclesiastical meaning, something ought to be said also about inquisitorial proceedings, which by themselves do not necessarily indicate concern with doctrine and moral guidance. For someone in a position to badger someone else, the inquisitorial style is good theater and gratifying to the ego. He who sits in judgment clothed in righteousness and ostensibly devoted to ultimate values appears impressive. Compared with goon squads and stuffing ballot boxes this is a classy style. Compared with planting lies in the press and tacking sneaky riders to legislation it is a classy style. Indignation will pass for probity. The manner can be assumed for short-run purposes: to ruin a personal enemy or rival, to grab the spotlight, to create a scapegoat for an industrial accident, a financial slump, a bungled military operation, and so on. The inquisitorial style with nothing behind it was the essence of McCarthyism. "Hatred of communism is like hatred of sin and error: a moral obligation" declared Aware, Inc., a satellite of the House Un-American Activities Committee. Impurity is easier to prove than wrongdoing.

For application to organizational behavior, social dynamics, and the transmission of ideas in the broadest sense, monopoly is the concept that illuminates heresy. The first aim of spiritual monopolists is to see that no religious experience occurs outside their domain. The status of sole supplier takes precedence over the quality and extent of services offered. Dissent from that principle, if it cannot be annihilated, must be branded not only wrong but irreligious. By the monopolists it is defined as experience that has passed out of the realm of religion. Thus a spiritual monopoly presents itself as a constituent part of what it trades in—in that sense not to be seen as a mediator only. For several decades in the United States, to cite an analogy from business, "the telephone company" was inseparable from the instrument in the minds of most people—the science and technology and physical network, the funding and management and protocol, the very existence of telephoning as a human activity.

Monopolists of course seek to corner a commodity or service which people with purchasing power are convinced they must have and are incapable of providing for themselves. In this regard spiritual monopolists possess an advantage over their counterparts in business. A monopoly in pepper or silicon chips is vulnerable to stealing and smuggling. It may be broken or transferred abruptly through the power of the state. Substitutes may be found that do the job better. If nothing else, life goes along pretty well without pepper or chips. Spiritual monopolists, however, begin with an enduring, compelling, and almost universal desire for an authentic connection with the sacred, and atop this practically indestructible base they can stimulate unlimited demand for satisfying the desire more intensely. The pool of potential competitors with the requisite vision is by nature small. A spiritual monopoly once in place cannot be superseded without costly emotional and social upheaval. In spiritual enterprise a strong design, a superior décor as it were, tends to retain influence even among dissenters, rivals, and supplanters. Poetically the Bible, intellectually the writings of the fathers, and dramaturgically the sacraments and edifices served this function in Christendom.

These theoretical advantages of spiritual monopolies over their business counterparts may nevertheless be offset by greater potential inefficiencies. Most business monopolies are inclined to avoid or cut off unprofitable customers. By contrast, given the goal of ensuring that no religion occurs outside their domain, spiritual monopolists insist upon automatic or compulsory enrollment of everyone within reach, and they define departure as a crime. The cost of hewing to this line can be ruinous. Between 1566 and 1654, at the height of its military prowess and as the leading Counterreformation power,

Spain was showered with gold and silver from the New World: the crown's share alone was worth 121 million ducats, the greatest treasure yet amassed in Europe. During the same period, however, the Spanish spent nearly twice that amount in a vain attempt to keep the Netherlands in the fold. For many business monopolies, the less customers know about operations—costs and profits, how salt reaches their tables, say, and oil lights their lamps—the better. Indifference to production in no way diminishes enthusiasm for consumption. Apathy makes a mockery of faith, however, and widespread apathy is what results if spiritual life consists of passive attendance. Consequently spiritual monopolists spend enormous zeal and effort to counteract the apathy they themselves cause.

To monopolize moral authority is wasteful in at least four other ways. Boring, frustrating, and malnourishing the subject population by trying to make them subsist exclusively on what the clergy produce, a monopoly in effect underwrites bootleg spirituality—folk cults, codes of honor, self-centered meditation, and so forth—the classic case of a poor product inefficiently policed at a high price. Monopoly draws sanctimonious bullies into the church and favors their promotion. Some of the spiritually gifted who also find places in the enterprise are converted into accomplices and bullies themselves, and some of the spiritually gifted are outlawed and destroyed simply for lack of a place. Perceived as a violation of moral authority, monopoly devalues whatever is achieved by those holding ecclesiastical office. In the eyes of many people it diminishes the credibility of moral authority in general.

What is prudent and what is expedient are two different things, however. Waste rarely bothers those in a position to pass the cost along or sweep it under the rug while extracting money for themselves or for an institution to which their fortunes are tied. Still less does waste matter, at least in the short run, where power is the object. A convenient source of revenue, available now, outweighs a hypothetically optimal system attainable in the future. And so monopolies do come into existence.

The utility of a monopolistic interpretation can be demonstrated in unraveling the case of Wang Hongwen, youngest of China's Gang of Four and to some Westerners an example of a man devoured by a monolithic ideology. An ecclesiastical inquisitor might indeed appreciate the air of rectitude surrounding Wang's arrest in 1976 for moral offenses, among them the sin of viewing capitalist films such as *The Count of Monte Cristo*. However, the inquisitorial style was merely a pretext for keeping him in storage for possible use by the new leaders —as an exemplary corpse perhaps, or someone to trade in case the henchmen he had put in office and the auxiliary forces he had created in the Red Guards proved hard to dislodge, or a source of information and denunciation for dislodging them, or a candidate for rehabilitation if the wind blew that way. Arrested by the Hua faction at a time when it was unclear which leaders and which policies would prevail, Wang was held without trial until 1980, when the Deng faction, now firmly in charge, sentenced him to life imprisonment. Morals and movies had nothing to do with it and were not mentioned again. Wang, a vice chairman of the Communist party at the time of his arrest, was basically convicted of being unfit for office. In the eyes of those who took power, he committed political blunders and illicit political acts, promoted policies and followers harmful to the country (and to those who supplanted him). According to a January 1988 Associated Press story, Wang may eventually be freed. If so, the government will be advertising magnanimity, power, and confidence all at the same time, by signaling that the foolish ideas of this insignificant person, who could have been squashed like a bug, pose no threat.

Thus heresy is not a helpful concept in tracing how a vice-chairman of the party and colleague of Mao's widow was reduced to the status of an unimportant jailbird. It is helpful, however, in understanding why in Russia the power of the state was brought to bear on an obscure poet with no political connections.

In 1937 the Soviet state security forces seized Varlam Shalamov, a young and virtually unknown poet. They had detected him saying a good word about the writings of the émigré novelist Ivan Bunin, and for this wickedness Shalamov was sentenced to seventeen years of forced labor in Siberia. That Stalin, a dictator with a genius for ruling by terror, should commit vast resources to a police network capable of inflicting massive punishment for the tiniest infraction by a harmless person is understandable. And in deciding whom to savage in order to frighten the rest, an obscure poet may well have seemed expendable, more useful for a display of cruelty than as a citizen. Yet why did a regime that could fabricate any charge it pleased go to extremes of doctrinal purity, maintaining a list of proscribed texts? Why did a notoriously anticlerical regime, whose leader asked sarcastically how many divisions the pope could send into combat, choose intellectual "error" as an official justification for harsh punishment? Cynicism, opportunism, sadism, and sheer chance may be necessary to explain Shalamov's fate, but they are not sufficient.

The Russian ruling class that formed under Stalin perhaps felt a greater need for exclusive moral authority than the Chinese group that consolidated around Mao. The Russians were bound by the same dogmatic belief that only a centralized revolutionary party may determine what is ideologically correct, but Hitler had not yet enabled them to tap deep reserves of nationalism as the Japanese were already doing for Mao. Nor was there in Russia a pervasive Confucian ethic that inculcated respect for order. Consequently a crazed, insecure drive for control was evident—utter insistence on the exclusive right to judge what might be written and read, an unrelenting claim to be a constituent part of the process of right thinking, recruitment of sanctimonious bullies, and other earmarks of exaggerated orthodoxy. Yet in Russia more than in most societies moral authority belongs to writers. From Pushkin to Solzhenitsyn, given the ossification of the church, the blunders, brutality, and immorality of successive governments, and the homicidal relations with neighboring countries, writers have stepped into the breach. Thus the new Russian ruling class doubly distrusted writers, often dismissed as "unreliable petty bourgeoisie." They were likely to shirk their Leninist duty to destroy the hegemony of old reactionary ideas with socially progressive literature. Worse, they were prone to become competitors. The logic of spiritual monopoly will not permit such a thing.

Yes and No:
The Sociology of Intellectuals

Such is the craving for respect that groups at the bottom of society or on the margin award it to themselves if necessary. Pariahs, workers in despised occupations, persecuted races and sects, slaves, prisoners, and outlaws usually develop furtive ways not only to resist their oppressors but also to glorify among themselves beliefs, characteristics, and practices of which the dominant class is ignorant or contemptuous. "Dirty" Gypsies and "sleazy" carnival roustabouts may convince themselves they belong to a chosen people, an exclusive club.

Given an opening, however, ingenious maneuvers will be carried out to gain respect from other groups. If all goes well, social standing and self-respect can be enhanced at the same time by announcing lofty goals. This is the dream of successful professions—to claim goals so lofty that in this messy world it is no disgrace to fall a bit short, so lofty in fact that only a superior group would espouse the goals in the first place.

Intellectuals, it appears, are adroit at such maneuvers on behalf of their group, especially in the modern period. Since the Enlightenment a striking ideal of the intellectual hero has been put forth in vivid imagery and an exalted tone against heavy odds. In 1784 Kant offered the motto *Sapere aude* (dare to know), by which he meant, as Peter Gay says, "take the risk of discovery, exercise the right of unfettered criticism, accept the loneliness of autonomy." Condorcet, mathematician and savant, declared that the death of Socrates had constituted "the first crime announcing the war between philosophy and superstition."

Jefferson wrote, "Nobody can conceive that nature ever intended to throw away a Newton upon the occupations of a crown." The abolitionist Wendell Phillips preached in the nineteenth century that the intellectual has "no object but truth—to tear a question open and riddle it with light." In addition to such explicit pronouncements there has been of course an outpouring of imaginative literature. Stendhal, Baudelaire, Ibsen, Mann, Joyce, and who knows how many other writers provide virtually a library on the trials and triumph of the intellectual hero. Even in the 1960s, hardly a time of measured prose, the American film critic Parker Tyler wrote that "the historical duty of the international avant-garde is to consider the poetic imagination in its keeping."

A composite of the ideal as it has come down in the United States and Europe would picture intellectuals as critical, sensitive truth-seekers who through their powers of insight, observation, conceptualization, expression, and creativity bring forth knowledge, forms, and values heretofore only latent in existence. On behalf of all humankind they burst through official interpretations of reality. They serve as theorists and heralds of justice and happiness. Powerful elements in society are hostile or indifferent to intellectuals. They may hang or starve these heroes, at least force them into unstable communities of the alienated. Ultimately, though, intellectuals hold out against persecution as a spiritual elite. The heroes and heroines may suffer doubts, weaken, make mistakes; but at their best they are indeed the ones who dare, who say No in thunder, who earn a place at the head of humanity's line of march. The dauntless thinker or artist enriches life with essential undertakings and values that would otherwise be lost.

Bohemia (of the Left Bank kind) deserves special mention as a setting created by the avant-garde. It kept visible what otherwise might have been put out of sight as inconvenient or criminal in the industrial state: the desire to experiment, to adhere to standards of craftsmanship, and to demonstrate, in Raymond Aron's words, "that the hierarchy of wealth and authority does not reflect the hierarchy of values." The genius of bohemia lay precisely in making these aspirations three-dimensional by occupying actual neighborhoods in actual capital cities, decking people in highly noticeable costumes, and openly breaking taboos. Ever in the wrong, the *New York Times* unwittingly revealed the success of bohemians in America by concluding in an editorial in 1858 that "it is not an encouraging sign for us that the tribe has become so numerous as to form a distinct and recognizable class."

In societies which could not afford or would not tolerate bohemians, a similar but more beleaguered collectivity formed. Aristocratic and church patronage—formerly the mainstay of intellectuals and seldom producing more of them than could be employed—dwindled in relation to the number of qualified aspirants. In any case such support was politically and psychologically distasteful to many intellectuals. They found themselves forming an intelligentsia—that is, a minority of enlightened thinkers and artists ground between a brutal ruling class that had no use for them and uncomprehending masses as likely as not to denounce them to the police. The locus classicus of this predicament was nineteenth-century Russia, where reportedly the term *intelligentsia* was put into circulation in the 1860s by the novelist Boborykin.

The university as it expanded and secularized after the Enlightenment also figured in the saga of the intellectual hero, although somewhat inadvertently. At a safe distance the university absorbed and diluted the advances of bohemia and the intelligentsia. It became a meeting place for the discontented young on a larger scale than before. The ceremonial right of professors to disagree served as a counterexample to the normal conditions of industrial work. Simply the nature of scholarship led to another healthy counterexample. In the face of bigness and centralization in so many spheres, complicated activities called the arts and sciences continued to be carried on by subdisciplinary groups small enough for the participants to know each other's work, correspond, and to a surprising degree meet face to face.

Autonomy and purity are stirring ideals. Certainly the ideal of the intellectual as romantic hero motivated a number of supremely talented people and became familiar in one stereotype or another to all social classes. The circumstances of intellectuals in modern society were desperate enough to make the mere conception of the ideal role audacious. Not only did aristocratic and ecclesiastical support shrink at the same time that it became more odious, but some new jobs, new goals, and new relationships opened up in such a way as to exclude intellectuals. Karl Polanyi in *The Great Transformation* reports that in Britain, "Telford, founder and lifelong President of the Society of Civil Engineers, refused membership in that body to applicants who had studied physics and, according to Sir David Brewster, never made himself acquainted with the elements of geometry." Ostentatious intellect was not the way to obtain a post in a growing number of "scientific" and "rational" endeavors such as the London metropolitan police system that replaced parish constables. Forward-looking German intellectuals were suspect when the Prussian regime unified the country. In France the struggle of intellectuals for a place in modern society had been raging more than a century before the word *intellectual* came into use, coined about the time of the Dreyfus affair. Even then the reactionary Auguste Barrès pleased a number of people by defining *un intellectuel* as "a cultivated individual without any mandate."

To the extent that recognition and employment did come, conditions were often harsh. Intellectuals found their "product" treated more than ever as a kind of fluctuating luxury commodity. A French literary journalist in Louis Philippe's day summed it up: "There are first-class items in intellect as in any other economy. They have their market price, like asphalt or Marseille soap. Spiritual rates shift in the same fashion as industrial rates." Under the ancien régime it had been touch and go whether intellectuals were classified as artisans or petty gentlemen, but in modern societies it was easier to get at them as scapegoats. The Soviet state classified intellectuals as brain workers. When Stalin gained power over a Russia four-fifths agricultural, however, he found them a handy group whose persecution could terrorize, implicate, and mollify others with minimal interruption of efforts to industrialize. In the West it became standard practice to blame troubles on intellectual "decadents" and "agitators."

Thus the picture of the intellectual hero was attractive for reasons good and bad. The role enterprise was amazing. So much must be admitted. Intellectuals proposed to make their skills and values the base for high standing. The only disagreement among themselves was tactical.

Quite a few intellectuals had no wish to belong to bohemia or to an intelligentsia. On the contrary, they wished to have servants, wear clean linen, be addressed as "sir," and receive invitations to dinner in the best homes. Some examples are notorious. Gibbon vainly wore a dress sword on all possible occasions. Jefferson doted on expensive wine. Dostoevsky recanted his liberal views. The Trevelyans, Huxleys, Darwins, and Cornfords of Britain, the Adamses, Jameses, and Lowells in the United States, possessed wealth and privileged connections. In light of what went on among less distinguished intellectuals, these people were exceptional in their accomplishments and good fortune but not in their social preferences. The authors of czarist tracts and papal bulls were also intellectuals. Austrian professors in the nineteenth century automatically held the rank of honorary colonel in the imperial army. Bohemia was out of the question for Boston's Fireside Poets. Well into the twentieth century, the historian Merle Curti pointed out, highly respectable psychologists declared "that the average mental age of American adults was thirteen years. Papers bristling with statistics 'proved' that colored people were hopelessly inferior. . . . And a journalist sounded a clarion call to the intellectuals because the whole white world was threatened by a rising tide of color!" An abstract rationale was provided for British manufacturers and financiers who found it more efficient in the 1820s to let workers fall into the machinery than to build safe mills and for the Russian managers in the 1920s who ordered workers shot to discourage absenteeism.

In short and insofar as a line can be clearly drawn, a number of intellectuals chose the other social posture expanded and perfected in modern times—the role of expert. Those who took this route had a better chance of obtaining bureaucratic and honorific posts, where the jobs were. It is true that technicians and promoters of official culture must let policymakers determine goals, but at least they have the ear of the powerful and resources with which to work. Expertise was not necessarily more self-serving than a stance of spiritual superiority. The case could be argued that the best way to get society at large to respect intellectual work is through visible honors and rewards to those who do it. The obvious rebuttal lies in the work turned out by those whose main concern is social security. In any event, for intellectuals as a social class, expertise was simply an alternative mode of role enterprise.

Once intellectuals had reattached themselves to society, either as experts or as superior spirits, the limitations of both roles became more conspicuous. In a world of more than fifty thousand technical journals and over a hundred thousand booklength research reports per year, much "intellectual" work is patently boondoggling. Ministries of propaganda and war the world over were able to buy plenty of brainy help. In disgust when this development was well along, Jacques Barzun consigned the term *intellectual* to "anyone who carries a briefcase." As with experts, so with "name" artists, adroit at manufacturing publicity. Emilio Marinetti, leader of the Futurist school of painting and poetry in Italy in the 1930s, for instance, issued a manifesto calling for a ban on pasta. Macaroni, he announced, was "a symbol of oppressive dullness, plodding deliberation, and fat-bellied conceit." The American Macaroni Manufacturers Association rose to the bait by sending a telegram of protest to Mussolini.

Efforts to enlist history in the social cause of intellectuals, understandable when they were fighting for a foothold, seemed less edifying when used to divert attention from their current failings or to hector rivals. At its crudest this took the form of referring not to any specific history but to a vague and magical past. Conservative intellectuals and radical intellectuals sounded almost alike in this mode. Writing from Paris in the 1920s, Julien Benda, a principled snob, maintained that he saw throughout history "an uninterrupted series of philosophers, men of religion, men of literature, artists, men of learning . . . whose influence, whose lives, were in direct opposition to the opportunism of the multitudes." Inflamed in the 1960s against phony liberals who staffed the military-industrial complex, Theodore Roszak wrote: "There was a time when men of intellect described the purpose of their lives in ways that stirred the souls of the noble and chilled the blood of the base."

A related form of historical shoddiness was to start with a presupposition and ransack the library for an illustration—any illustration, from any period or culture—to "prove" it. If you believed that intellectuals above all aspire to be mandarins and when successful act as callously as any other members of a ruling class, you emphasized out of context an item such as the following, extracted from H. R. Trevor-Roper's study of European witch-hunting on the eve of the Scientific Revolution. "Nicholas Rémy was a cultivated scholar, an elegant Latin poet, the devoted historian of his country. When he died in 1616, having sent (we are told) between two and three thousand victims to the stake, he was universally respected." If on the contrary you believed that intellectuals are dedicated to free inquiry even at the risk of their own privileges and person, you extracted from the history of science the case of Shen Kua. Shen (born A.D. 1030) belonged to the upper level of the Chinese scholar-gentry: at various times serving as ambassador, supervisor of waterworks (roughly equivalent to serving in the contemporary U.S. on the board of the Federal Reserve system), and director of an academy. He is better remembered by sinologists, however, as the author of a treatise on geography, geology, agronomy, and other "low" concerns. The work was written in time stolen from official duties, and only 10 of its 584 sections dealt with what orthodox Chinese intellectuals deemed worthy of their attention.

The use of an emblematic name to stand for values supposedly realized in the past combined the two kinds of historical shoddiness. To use the name of a historical person implies concreteness without demonstrating knowledge of the individual's actual life. Confucius? He thought wise thoughts, or at least was thought by the ancient Chinese to think them, and that's that. At the same time an emblematic name confers the sweep of generalization without stating any. By implication the name Napoleon, for instance, has been made to stand for vague ideas of military genius, self-defeating ambition, the compensating drive of short men, et cetera. Such names are learned and passed along as rhetoric rather than history. They have floated free of their biographical and historical moorings.

Unfortunately many modern intellectuals continued to use for their emblem a name encrusted with tradition—that of Socrates. With all of history to rifle, they could have found a thousand superior models. Even in the ever-murky present, even in one's own vicinity (if Noam Chomsky, say, is a neighbor), better candidates than Socrates exist. The actual Socrates, as distinct from Plato's beautiful fiction, was a man of few intellectual accomplishments and monumental bad judgment who probably martyred himself in hopes of posthumous celebrity.

From the writings of Aristophanes, Xenophon, Plato, and shortly afterward the writings of Aristotle, it appears that Socrates' social theories would have made Athens a worse place. In contrast to the ideal of participation by free citizens in the *polis* as the highest form of communal life, he advocated rule by a despot—"the one who knows"—toward whom even "impertinence" was illegitimate. Socrates opposed elected executives. He opposed lawmaking by assemblies, whose members he called "dunces and weaklings." He opposed jury trials. He opposed education except for male aristocrats. As long as any such institutions had to be borne at all, he desired participation to be restricted to a small circle of oligarchs, and he recommended that men of intellect (no women need apply) avoid civic affairs altogether as irredeemably "petty." By way of an admirable contrast to the way things were done in Athens, he praised Sparta and Crete among existing states. They enforced a caste system, operated a secret police, restricted travel in and out, and excluded philosophy and theater.

It also appears that Socrates' protégés really did make Athens a worse place. Alcibiades, portrayed as "charming" in Plato's Socratic dialogues, was a profligate who sold his military services to Sparta (Athens's chief enemy at the time) and initiated the oligarchic tyranny of 411 B.C. This regime promoted aristocratic secret clubs that assassinated political opponents. Critias, another one-time student, led the Tyranny of the Thirty in 404 B.C., which welcomed a Spartan garrison into Athens and paid three hundred bullies to patrol the streets with whips. According to Xenophon, fifteen hundred Athenians were murdered by the Thirty in eight months, almost as many as were killed in the final decade of the Peloponnesian War.

Although Socrates held no office under the Thirty and received no honors from them, neither did he complain or leave the city. His passiveness was probably compounded of his theories (according to which the Thirty were not autocratic enough), what he deemed expedient for himself, and indifference to the suffering of others. He expressed no regret over the loss of citizenship by Athenian craftsmen and traders after two hundred years or the widespread confiscation of property by the Thirty. Immediately after their overthrow and the negotiation of a remarkably prudent amnesty, he resumed his antidemocratic teaching.

In return for damning their institutions and beliefs and praising their enemies Socrates produced little for the Athenians in the way of intellectual value. When pressed to describe "the one who knows" or to say what was known, he, as A. J. Ayer observes of Voltaire, "subsides into talk of the weakness of our understanding." Linguistically naive in the extreme, he equated philosophy with definition and in practice worked at punching holes in others' definitions without providing any himself.

In all likelihood Socrates courted his execution. He was seventy years old and dreaded sickness and old age. Discredited, he could not expect to attract many new students or to figure any longer as a lovable curmudgeon in drama—the contemporary equivalent of media attention. As I. F. Stone points out in *The Trial of Socrates*, he forewent his best and most obvious legal defense: the argument that the death penalty was not prescribed for the offenses with which he was charged. Although 220 jurors out of 500 voted for acquittal, with boasting and mockery he managed to turn more of them against him and to insult the judges in preparation for sentencing. In Plato's account the means to escape and take honored refuge in another city were available but refused by Socrates on the grounds that he must not break the law even to save his life from an unjust verdict. If the story is true in some measure, the high-mindedness at least is doubtful; for here was a teacher who had advised philosophers not even to read the laws. Possibly Socrates sought death in despair—a bitter, ailing old man who felt nothing for his wife and children and who was humiliated by the failure as well as the excesses of his students. Possibly he sought death in the spirit of a childish egotist who would show the Athenian majority what a noble soul he possessed, and then they would be sorry. But possibly he struck a deal with like-minded younger men to make his martyrdom serve the oligarchic cause while procuring him fame. Still another possibility is that Plato seized that opportunity on his own. More politic than Socrates, he lay low till tempers cooled, then ran a highly successful academy for many years. His Socratic dialogues incidentally tried to rehabilitate the reputation of Critias, Plato's murderous cousin, and his uncle Charmides, another collaborator with the Spartans. It will never be known exactly who intended what, but in effect Plato became either the world's greatest literary executor or the world's greatest cover-up artist.

The use of Socrates' name century after century thus seems to contain no lesson except the trivial one that intellectuals are as ingenuous and disingenuous as everyone else. The actual life of Socrates may teach that conceiving intellectuals to be refined spirits at odds with the status quo does not necessarily result in good intellectual work or keep them from doing harm. Yet that too is a weak lesson. In almost any culture on record, individual cases can be found to slant the conclusion either way. The sum of what intellectuals did in specific situations may not add up to a clear pattern, let alone a balance. As one cuts across groups and cultures and eras, it becomes all the more likely that generalizations about the social position of intellectuals are inherently limited in explanatory power. It happens, for example, that intellectuals as a social type tend to stand nearer to the top of society than to the bottom, and on the average they tend to be more analytical about the status quo than other groups at about the same level. So what? Social position is a poor predictor of merit.

The traditional Chinese scholar-gentry, for instance, customarily referred to as *shen-shih*, are the supreme test of what happens when intellectuals as a class are recruited carefully, stationed high, and granted a monopoly. They turn out not to differ greatly from poets starving in the garrets of Paris. Collectively, they do both well and poorly.

By the time of the T'ang Dynasty, established in A.D. 618, the Confucians had regularized the examinations through which the overwhelming majority of individuals who belonged to the scholar-gentry gained admission. Special hats, robes, and trimmings were reserved for them, and commoners were required to address them as "Excellency." Not nearly all *shen-shih* (making up, with wives and minor children, about 1.3 percent of the population in the late nineteenth century) were state officials, and not all high officials were gentry; yet *shen-shih* generally had the resources both to cultivate the arts and sciences privately and to play a part in public life. Since local administration often fell to them whether they were formally enrolled in the imperial service or not, scholars normally took part in collecting taxes (from most of which they were themselves exempt), amassing grain for public stores, licensing gambling, and lending money.

On the whole this privilege and cohesion produced no better results than the individualism of Socrates. With less reason to fear it, the *shen-shih* attacked intellectual competition. They drove Taoists and Buddhists not only out of office but out of sight. On one occasion a Ming prince—in flight from an uncle who had seized the throne and in need of the deepest obscurity the society could provide for a literate man—concealed himself for years by becoming a monk. Women were categorically barred from sitting for degrees, as were actors, musicians, and dancers. Architects, art dealers, military and hydraulic engineers, physicians, and scribes were often well connected politically but seldom belonged to the gentry. Military officers took practical examinations and were well rewarded but regarded as coarse. The greatest collections of Chinese texts were gathered for the purpose of burning offending works.

The *shen-shih* wasted a good deal of the brainpower they monopolized. The typical intellectual career consisted of preparing for and taking sterile examinations on nine ancient ethico-literary works. The sinologist David Nivison maintains that candidates at each level of examinations "had to be prepared to distort or even invent meaning in the assigned text." In Ming times the exact number of characters in which a scholar might couch an essay-answer was sometimes prescribed. The historian Chang Chung-li reported the case of a man who climbed to the top rank of the gentry by spending "35 years preparing for examinations and 160 days in the examination hall itself."

On the average, then, the mandarin was no more impressive than the Socratic outsider. More to the point, however, he was not necessarily less impressive either. Ku Yen-wu, a seventeenth-century literatus who flourished under the same system, argued brilliantly that the examinations were worse than sterile. In his opinion they actually taught and inculcated bad writing and feeble thinking. The relation between social position and intellectual results remains vague.

Quite possibly more can be gleaned about the behavior of intellectuals by considering their character rather than their social position. As Erich Fromm said: "Gratification results from behavior in accordance with character." Instead of letting the label "intellectual" stand for total identity and affixing the label by social criteria, it might be better to analyze the preferences and actions of people who, whatever other strands are woven into their identity, gravitate toward intellectual pursuits. Aside from immediate ends they take pleasure in conceptions and mental permutations as such. They enjoy putting ideas "out there" where those ideas can be inspected, copied, elaborated, opposed, retired, or renewed. They prize the choice of forms, materials, and contexts through which values are presented. They have a passion for symbols that codify a great deal of experience and that in themselves become objects of consciousness. There is a stock character that *chooses* to engage in the intellectual process.

Certainly for weighing intellectual products, social identification by itself is primitive. "Priestcraft" may be a common way for intellectuals to elevate themselves and mystify others, but awareness of the maneuver is inadequate for confronting a building, a parable, a system of logic put forth under the auspices of this or that priesthood. The Polish philosopher Leszek Kolakowski succinctly criticized the reductionist naiveté of dwelling on social origins alone: "Although moral values and behavior are determined by upbringing, tradition, membership in social groups, and zeitgeist, knowledge of the determining conditions does not establish the truth or falseness of the values accepted. The fact that a person judges something to be good or bad because circumstances inclined him to do so does not mean this something is good or bad."

Consequently in addressing the problem of the intellectual in modern society it may be well to expend less passion on unmasking mandarins and exposing radicals. Intellectuals have arrived—they always do. But some never departed, and some never returned. Some are trivialized, and some are made into scapegoats. Social identification has fueled splendid polemics and scattered nuggets of wisdom. (The comedian Mort Sahl in a way captured the 1980s with his quip that it was a time when professionals and intellectuals lined up to sell in.) Yet the utility of social identification remains modest. Sooner or later a mandarin will unaccountably risk his or her neck to condemn the emperor. Meanwhile a Socrates will be caught faking integrity.

The question is whether the place where all now mingle is a place where anyone ought to be, especially if intellect is the issue. A few years ago the physicist Gerald Holton drew attention to a startling effect of "scientific" specialization. For perhaps the first time in history, he pointed out, large numbers of intellectuals cannot construct a picture of the world. The problem seems to be to make the world whole enough so that human capacities, including intellectual capacity, are usable again.

The Great Language Panic

Even in ancient times, as suggested by the myth of the Tower of Babel, there must have been glimmerings of language as a strange construction. A smart neolithic captive or go-between was in a position to notice that although each tongue purported to accommodate everything sayable, certain things voiced in one could not be expressed in another. Classical rhetoricians at times verged on treating truth as a plastic, optional element, a variable incorporated to suit linguistic design. Some traditional philosophers who composed conundrums and paradoxes evidently believed they were probing substantive questions. Yet others gave the impression of playing with language or, like prisoners mocking their keepers, of freeing themselves in spirit from linguistic confines by carrying the rules to absurdity.

By and large, however, before the modern period normal adult speakers experienced no chronic confusion or sense of futility over language. Peoples who suffered language doubts usually had good reason: they were disastrously misled and/or their world, including their language, was invaded by conquerors. In quieter times, large numbers were calm about possible limitations of language because they believed that through rituals, dreams, omens, and trances access could be had where language did not reach. Even as late as Kant, with his unperturbed distinction between apprehension and things as they are in themselves, there was not the modern nervousness about possible exclusion from a plenitude of being beyond words.

Traditional distrust of language had mostly to do with the *source* of an utterance. Notions of false prophecy and speakers possessed by demons are probably older than writing. Enemies in war and politics, it was understood, might say anything. The seducer, the thief, the trader, and the trickster (who figures frequently in folk literature) aimed to deceive. The simpleton, the apprentice, and the barbarian blundered. Originating from a "good" source or a "bad" source, texts were assumed to preserve a fixed identity over indefinite periods through any number of redactions. That people could err, lie, offend, exploit, digress, and contradict themselves was taken for granted—the fallibility of source. But the availability in principle of a right way to say the right thing in some absolute sense was seldom doubted.

In the West it was accepted that the order of the world could be truthfully represented in an order of words. As a first step, thoughts were presumed to derive from reality. As thoughts occurred, words were chosen to express them. Properly formed thoughts expressed in properly chosen words corresponded to reality—principal words substantively and auxiliary words by maintaining the traffic patterns that helped principal words to function.

Proto-modern friction between religion and science, the kind that caused trouble for Galileo and Descartes, did not essentially disturb traditional faith in language. Disputation was an old form. Conflict over ecclesiastical authority was an old problem, long since embedded in language in such terms as *schism* and *Joachite* (referring to the Cistercian monk Joachim of Floris, whose assertion that the church hierarchy would become superfluous got him placed in Heaven by Dante and censured posthumously by the Fourth Lateran Council in 1215). After the rage, slaughter, and cleavage of the Reformation, in fact, a way was found for a time to soften the conflict between religion and science. Namely, the idea of a clockwork universe took hold. No longer was God seen as a superhuman foreman measuring every furrow, inspecting every hem, directing the loading of every wagon. Rather, an awesome chief engineer was predicated, once and for all organizing the forces, materials, and values of the cosmos into a machine that ran itself with precision and regularity through natural laws, though of course God might intervene if he chose. In the eighteenth century, dissenters, deists, anticlericals, and materialists opposed bishops, conventional morality, and claims of revelation but did not find these unintelligible.

By the middle of the nineteenth century, however, the number of confusing episodes and productions in intellectual life began to mount up. (1) The new geology and what would become paleontology threw the traditional sense of time out of kilter. Archaeology, uncovering evidence of complex and unknown or dimly remembered civilizations, threw the sense of history into doubt. Darwin's *Origin of Species* (1859) put the sense of life and how it operated into question. Anthropology, beginning the inventory of cultures that would reveal several thousand ways of living and speaking but few universals, upset the sense of human nature.

Although much was said at the time and has been ever since about the blow delivered by science to traditional religion, the blow given by late-nineteenth-century and early-twentieth-century science to earlier *scientific* orthodoxy should be emphasized as well. Mathematics, mechanics, experimentation, inductive reasoning, chemistry, and systematic classification advanced significantly in the seventeenth and eighteenth centuries, so that a man born in Jefferson's time could feel he lived in an erudite era. A hundred years later, not only was much scientific knowledge superseded, but puzzles were developing as to how scientific explanation per se was conceivable. Statements and calculi might be governed not by what they purport to represent but by syntactic rules. "For it is easy to think and talk without the image of anything at all present to the mind," wrote William James; "words—the bare familiar sounds ending in *-tion* or *-ity* or *-ness*—will keep thoughts moving and make the thinker feel rational though he literally does not know what he is talking about."

(2) Relationships between corruption and beauty had of course been considered for millennia, sometimes in a puritanical spirit and sometimes with regret over mutability, and Baudelaire was scarcely the first poet to live a tormented life. *Les Fleurs du mal* (1857) came as a shock, however. The merging of beauty and evil and the raising of anxiety to a spiritual principle carried readers over the threshold of modern art. Henceforth artists were challenged to create boldly

original and exquisitely wrought forms for chaotic experiences and disclosures.

(3) French and German scholars like Alfred Loisy and Heinrich Holtzmann embarked on a program of biblical criticism that tended to dissolve Scripture into segments written by different hands. Folk motifs, root words, and tropes from neighboring cultures; sectarian quarrels; passages more incoherent than inspired—exhaustive attention to items such as these led toward reading the Bible as raw material for philology and anthropology.

(4) Two supreme unmaskers entered the scene at this time, Marx and Nietzsche. Marx branded "proper" language as a government informer. Standard definitions and locutions, cherished texts and genres, and learned explanations of the world amounted to no more than an act put on in the courtroom by a dirty little tool of the regime. This deceitful figure, trusted by no one, lacked even the dignity of an independent evildoer. Language could play only a pat role in the machinations of a ruling class to stay on top.

To Nietzsche, social class itself was a detail. Life as he painted it was saturated with contention and selfish urges, from infantile howls through the entire range of individual ambition and every possible coalition to grand theories designed to seize control of explanation itself. He insisted that language chiefly obscures: events happen unperceived unless they suit what words are prepared to recognize as fact. His own performance in language was disturbing, like much modern literature. A manic author out of nowhere found stark, agile language with which to violate and bewilder. After this unpleasant surprise, what guarantee could there be that language would not run off or turn on its handlers like a vicious animal?

Thus novel and threatening implications had been released into the atmosphere: human beings do not know what they are talking about, language immobilizes consciousness for the sake of word order, and speaking is inherently a contaminated act. It is one thing to say with cool hindsight that anxiety results when the rest of culture changes at a higher speed than language—a conspicuous feature of modernity. It was another thing to endure terrible stress at a time when clouds of confusion about language compounded the damage and shock. After World War I there was a widespread sense of disabled speakers and disfigured words.

The classic passage was written by Hemingway in *A Farewell to Arms:*

> I was always embarrassed by the words sacred, glorious, and sacrifice and the expression in vain. We had heard them, sometimes standing in the rain almost out of earshot, so that only the shouted words came through, and had read them, on proclamations that were slapped up by billposters over other proclamations, now for a long time, and I had seen nothing sacred, and the things that were glorious had no glory and the sacrifices were like the stockyards at Chicago if nothing was done with the meat except to bury it. There were many words that you could not stand to hear and finally only the names of places had dignity. Certain numbers were the same way and certain dates and these with the names of the places were all you could say and have them mean anything.

This does not read quite like traditional laments and disillusionment after a smash-up. An ambitious novelist seeking public acclaim, almost by definition committed to faith in the efficacy of words, made it a point of honor to write in a minimal style. Although he was a survivor speaking for troops of slaughtered men, he emphasized language as the casualty. Evidently sizable numbers of people felt that they had no words for their experience and that the words they had were no good.

Among those alarmed by the threatened collapse of language, the bunker intellectual was one type who appeared after the war. Convinced that language had proved to be inadequate, unreliable, and illusory, bunker intellectuals sought a fortified position on an isolated promontory where they could hold off verbal laxity, preserving only the barest, purest essentials of rational utterance. Two attitudes characterized bunker intellectuals, a command mood and a mood of resentment. They took pride in leaving excess baggage and abandoning the ordinary linguistic countryside, scorching what they could as they withdrew. No point in defending for sentimental reasons halfway positions that would be overrun anyway. Within the bleak strongholds they created, they vowed to live austerely and vigilantly. That was the command mood. In their resentful mood, bunker intellectuals dwelt on the egregious pretensions of language, the foolish mischief it abetted, and most of all how it had let them down.

The bunker intellectual of 1930, usually a he, believed in his heart of hearts that equations were the ideal form of utterance. Out of physical, social, and emotional necessity humans spent an unfortunate amount of their time at lower levels, and language reflected this through a messy history, irrational idioms, arbitrary usage, expressive impulses, and scandalous lapses into ambiguity, contradictions, fallacies, and incoherence. Nevertheless, that we find comfort in talking, that language more or less serves practical purposes and provides partial understanding, is no excuse for impurity at the highest level. Better to construct systems in which all terms are defined, all operations specified, all relationships consistent. In other words, void problems of reference and agency by making up artificial micro-languages that refer to nothing and that no one speaks. So that such systems would have a place to exist, science and measurement were permitted to hypothesize a world.

A. J. Ayer was a prime example of a bunker commander. In *Language, Truth, and Logic* (1936) he asserted that only one sort of utterance was worthy: words formed grammatically into an indicative sentence subject to analytical or empirical verification. By analytic he meant a deliberate tautology that starts with an a priori definition and proceeds through the operation of specified symbolic rules to reach a purely formal self-confirmation. By empirical he meant a proposition that could be tested against sense data. Other forms of utterance—stories and songs, jokes, advice, and questions, for example—were so much expressive noise. They might be of interest behaviorally, but they were not acceptable propositions. Against sentimentalists and backsliders who hoped somehow to preserve harmony between the order of words and the order of things, he was adamant:

> The proposition that a material thing cannot be in two places at once is constantly invoked by those who desire to prove that it is possible for an empirical proposition to be logically certain. But a more critical inspection shows that it is not empirical at all, but

linguistic. It simply records the fact that, as the result of certain verbal conventions, the proposition that two sense-contents occur in the same visual or tactile sense-field is incompatible with the proposition that they belong to the same material thing.

Having let his readers know the strict standards by which language was to be judged, Ayer covered several forms of discourse that he considered especially reprehensible. He came down hard on mysticism and metaphysics for their senseless and unintelligible efforts to "express the inexpressible." Like all bunker intellectuals he disdained "value judgments." On the one hand, since they are not acceptable propositions, "the question of truth or falsehood does not here arise." On the other hand, he was willing to concede that "moral experience" might be a fit subject for "the science of psychology or sociology," although without curiosity as to what this "science" consisted of. Under his standard disqualifier, "a cry of pain or a word of command is unverifiable—because they do not express genuine propositions."

Philosophically, the bunker intellectuals made rather a mess of science by defining it as a set of procedures for confirming which sentences about which sensed things are true. Sensation was an incomplete link between consciousness and things in view of the scientific doctrine that no sensation of sensation occurs. They ignored the scientific theory that the actions of an observer alter the phenomenon under observation. They showed little interest in discriminating among the many disciplines lumped under the label "science," paid no attention to the passions and competition of scientists, and seemed to assume that changes in procedure always represented "progress."

Interestingly, several bunker intellectuals who were actually versed in science outgrew the bunker. Bertrand Russell was one. Without relaxing his vigilance toward such linguistic difficulties as "illegitimate totalities," he broadened his concerns to include the point that science could be subordinated by the state as easily as language. Wittgenstein in his late phase inclined to argue that meanings manifested themselves directly in the exterior world. A man is doing arithmetic, he thought, if the right signs appear on his pad, and no linguistic or chemical analysis is required to further certify it.

Not all who stayed in the bunker were austere logicians. Michel Foucault, the best-known recent exemplar of resentment toward language, did not capture the attention of the reading public until the end of the 1960s, but he followed in the footsteps of Marx and Nietzsche, who had created a genre of unmasking and a profession of unmasker as a by-product of their brilliant performance. Indifferent to circumscribed truth tests, Foucault dramatized the vice, treachery, and repression concealed in language.

In his diatribes language was accused of screening the world from consciousness, diverting attention to itself. If we were not duped by language, he complained, we would see a beautiful "nomadic and dispersed multiplicity" out there, pure events instead of a "dreary succession of the identical." Dominant groups everywhere, he was keen on pointing out, shape language to justify their power and silence opposition. "Humanity installs each of its violences in a system of [linguistic] rules and thus proceeds from domination to domination." *Combat* was his term for the making of scientific theories, schools of art, and systems of logic.

To give Foucault his due, he stood up pretty well to a problem that every philosopher of disjunction faces—framing an affirmative generalization that holds constant across a world defined as a plenum of fluid differences. Suppress categories and the axiom of univocality, he argued, and ontology is still possible through the subsistence of recurrence. Events may not share an identity, but they continue to happen; reality continues to occur. ". . . In the same stroke, both the dice and the rules are thrown. . . ." Foucault's acuity in this regard, however, probably for himself as well as his readers, was coincidental to making language look vile.

Rigidity and morbid suspicion permeated the bunker. Ordinary language was restricted to authorized areas and admitted only during visiting hours with a monitor present at all times. The distrust that established such rules in the first place combined with the tension of living under them to give words the exaggerated importance of sex in a convent school. Imaginations were inflamed with the prospect of what awful things might be going on outside the bunker.

As a matter of fact, what had happened outside the bunker was that millions of people found more casual ways to avoid being taken in by language. Disposable language, machine language, and the use of sublinguistic social noises served the purpose.

Disposable language, increasingly popular as the twentieth century wore on, offered the same ego protection as sleeping around. Risks of commitment, rejection, and disillusionment were minimized. Dependence was lowered through surfeit rather than deprivation. Under a strategy of disposable language words are drawn effortlessly as though from a box of Kleenex: cheap, plentiful, interchangeable, available in plain or designer style. Except for someone in the tissue business or with an urgent need to wipe, to *respond* to Kleenex would be absurd. In a world of disposable language "crisis situation" is as good as "crisis." Can you guess the meaning of "could care less"? It means "could not care less." "Whatever." Be understood or not. Pick offhand from vocabularies and idioms at the take-out counter. Toss words around or stack them for such formal occasions as legal documents. "Spokespersons" hustle up new ways to deceive, mislead, and impress, but the public hears only the drone of manager talk, one phrase the same as another unless the humming is far off-key. Caspar Weinberger had the governing-class touch: "precision-guided" for "aim." David Stockman was in over his head: "I sat back concussed."

Another way of devaluing language was to shift faith to apparatus. Let the propaganda, jargon, canned entertainment, media babble, and empty exchanges flow by. What counts are machines and networks for pumping the words, pictures, and numbers. Machines and networks flatter the ego like language; for we invented them too, and they can be *owned*. Hence the fascination with dial-back telephones that communicate with answering machines, memos written mostly in order to put them through word processors, teams of technicians operating billion-dollar satellite equipment for live coverage of staged events, disks that store the addresses of people who have no interest in being addressed.

Still another way of evading language was to substitute pseudo-verbal social noises in greater proportion. All-purpose noises were nothing new, but their use increased as language lost authority. A few decades back, architectural masterpieces were "swell," meatloaf sandwiches were "swell," graduation from college was "swell," and a new desk blotter at the office was "swell." Lately, such set gestures as thumbs-up have been heavily worked with tags on the order of "you know" and "really." Grunts, squeaks, moans, and whoops carry a heavier semantic load.

When a toddler manages to say "Da Da" by way of comment on a TV shaving-cream commercial, the performance is admirable. He or she has seen a connection between the image on the screen and the people at home, has found a promising way to please those on whom a child's immediate welfare depends, and has made the strenuous effort cognition requires without much language to help. How to take grownups who go (or remain) primitive is not so clear. In the following examples the "explainers" could be withholding their feelings and thoughts, or they could know nothing. They could be putting themselves over as moxie people with a healthy independence from verbiage, or they could be faking a social transaction to slide by.

Situation. A woman in the next office spoke sharply on the phone.
Explanation. She went bullshit!

Situation. A neighbor killed himself and his wife and children last night.
Explanation. He went bullshit!

Situation. Unable to prevent a certain alliance from forming, the president publicly welcomed it. However, someone leaked news of his secret hostility and dissembling to the press. He and his advisors stay up late arguing whether to plant a story discrediting the leak. Possibly the allied parties are too cynical to be ruffled by what they assumed to be bad faith anyway. In that case, why risk a second leak exposing the planted story? On the other hand, what if . . .
Explanation. They went bullshit!

In the long run humans do not bear up well without meaning, and meaning passes through language. Thus the drawback of these popular evasions. Edgy, transient meaning is all that can be expected from disposable language, comparable to living on the streets. Through machines meaning can be dubbed just as songs and laughter are dubbed (with the same hollow results), just as photographs and statistics are faked. Though argot and pretended stupidity may be better than no resistance, minimal language loses meaning. "Truncheons are for louts," observed Richard Mitchell in *Less Than Words Can Say* (1979). "The great masters of social manipulation . . . know . . . that the establishment of a flexible and subtle language for the ruling classes is only half of what's needed. The other half is the perpetuation of an ineffective and minimal language among the subjects."

Those in the grip of the great modern language panic reacted hysterically to those who were immune. All through the time of distrust, certain strong spirits such as William James, Edward Sapir, and Noam Chomsky were advancing the understanding of language profoundly. "The normal person," Sapir serenely took for granted, in contrast to the bunker intellectuals' strained maneuvers, "is never convinced by the mere content of speech." E. E. Cummings charmingly represented the writer's relationship to language through the metaphor of the lion tamer. Congressman Maury Maverick of Texas had a moment of triumph over language through language with the word *gobbledygook*. Such people engaged confidently with language were seen by the panicky as sounding the alarm or themselves a cause for alarm.

Relativism, to recall one famous example that became a bugaboo for the panicky, was seized on as conclusive proof that language is deceptive and inadequate. Actually, Benjamin Whorf, widely cited by the distrustful, had ventured a rather mild statement while he was still more of a chemical engineer (his original profession) than a linguist. "We are thus introduced to a new principle of relativity, which holds that all observers are not led by the same physical evidence to the same picture of the universe, unless their linguistic backgrounds are similar or can in some way be calibrated." Under Sapir's tutelage, after serious fieldwork in ethnography, and through his own driving intelligence, Whorf came to think of relativity as a robust, salutary principle. One's native tongue stood to language as a traveler's phrasebook stands to an unabridged dictionary. Instead of the few small and necessarily sloppy mental experiments that a single culture-bound intellectual could carry out, one had access through the abundance of languages to viewpoints perfected by whole peoples over many generations under "real" conditions. To explore the consequence of viewing existence as event, for instance, talk to the Nootka of Vancouver Island, who possessed an "all-verb" language.

Under the impression that he had brought bad news, Whorf's readers tried to punish him. The principle of linguistic relativism is tautologous, they said, if the only evidence offered of a world view is linguistic. Yes, indeed—except that Whorf referred in his ethnography to such nonverbal phenomena as the kind of grain cultivated by a given people. Even with regard to labeling behavior, which he was one of the first to discuss, Whorf paid attention to the consequences of reacting to signs as well as the fact *of* reacting to them. The point about smoking around what are labeled "empty gasoline drums," in one of his examples, is that empty drums contain explosive vapors and are therefore more dangerous than filled drums.

Amplitude of experience, thought, and knowledge through language—vastly enriched opportunities to order the world and multiply meaning—went further still with Whorf's mentor, Edward Sapir. Reportedly Sapir knew German, French, English, Latin, and Sanskrit; several Semitic languages and several Sinitic ones; a dozen or more American Indian languages and at least one West African language. The mental experiments improvised by monolingual thinkers seemed crude to him compared with the distinctions and patterns one could observe ready-made in a plural world. His own mental experiments were elegant, as when he estimated that "the highly synthetic and periodic structure of Eskimo would more easily bear the weight of Kant's terminology than his native German." So little was he bothered by the "threat" of relativity that he viewed it as a handy aid to remind the linguist not to be "taken in by the forms of his own speech."

Prior to the language panic, grammar had been conceived as a set of explicit rules and procedures for putting words in the right order to represent the order of the world. Basics could be drilled into the young, and the finer points provided intellectual sport. Through grammar a flick of the reins—as in the distinction between "doing good" and "doing well"—guided language wherever one wanted to go. However, if all human groups interpreted the world through language and incompatible interpretations were what resulted, perhaps this said more about language than about the world. As scrutinized by modern linguists, grammar insidiously and inescapably caused gaps greater than "different ways of life." The grammar of a given language—and all natural grammars were of equal fixity, according to Sapir—forced speakers to include with their statements assumptions that overrode what they were trying to say. In English, for example, a formless extensional entity called "matter" is assumed behind every concrete subtype such as "coffee" that gives matter actual existence. In itself a mass noun, coffee must then be individualized, as in "pound of coffee" and "cup of coffee," when an instance of it appears in the world. "Matter" as such appears only in thought. Hopi language, by contrast, admits no formless extensional entities. One always speaks of "a" coffee, "a" water, and so forth, with the degree of generality indicated through the verb or predicator; but the speaker cannot help but express a degree of intensity or duration, an entity or at least quality that lies behind coffee like "matter" in English.

Many conventional parsers could not face their loss of power over grammar and never did give in to structural linguistics, which took a generation or two to establish itself. What the linguists said about grammar of course confirmed the deepest fears of the unmaskers and bunker intellectuals, who refused to explore nonverbal encounters as another way of coming at the world and who never made allowance for the dependent aspects of override. The only outlet for the assumptions buried in grammar, which itself makes no direct reference to the world, came through speakers: beings with intentions toward and connections with the world. Grammar rode piggyback or not at all.

Thus when Noam Chomsky in the 1950s and 1960s hypothesized that the capacity for conscious thought may follow from language acquisition, he inspired terror and willful misreading. His critics, grasping at any child-development studies that could be distorted to ward off the evil, as they saw it, of a brain nurtured by language, in effect drove him to add a "semantical component" so that they would cease "disproving" him by concocting sentences that were grammatically correct but senseless. Such readers of Chomsky ignored his emphasis on the creativity possible through language, which he took the trouble to trace back as a theory to the seventeenth century. They overlooked his express judgment that people possess cognitive abilities that are not linguistic. They passed over in silence Chomsky's qualified confidence in the referential power of language. A sentence, he speculated, may be the best picture, image, or diagram that can be given of a phenomenon.

Distance and hindsight make it possible to see that distrust of language was rising by the middle of the nineteenth century. There was a certain logic in the subsequent spreading panic, although no completely predetermined chain of events led inevitably to the "you know" epidemic of the 1970s. Without distance and hindsight, it is hard to say whether anxieties about language are becoming less acute as the end of the twentieth century approaches. Presumably the recovery of nerve will be uneven and indistinct until it is well along.

A recent change of mood among literary critics may be a sign that the worst is over. Considering that critics could not avoid dealing with works of verbal art, they coped prudently with language panic in the first place. Just when so many people felt let down, in the interval from Matthew Arnold to Northrop Frye, the critics became minor culture heroes, a catch for dinner parties and for semipopular periodicals. In part the F. R. Leavises, Lionel Trillings, and Allen Tates sidestepped language by talking of traditions, structures, symbols, and myths—anything but words. When I. A. Richards, who did talk about words, praised literature as "utterance of the whole soul," he made it sound different from and better than language. Bunker intellectuals remained skeptical, of course, but they could appreciate the tense engagement of modern critics with ambiguity and complexity. The successors of the New Critics actually climbed into the bunkers, many of which had fallen into disuse after the waning of logical positivism, and showed with their theories of structuralism and deconstruction that they could seal them as tightly as anybody. Jacques Derrida and his followers, to name one group, overshot the mark. By pronouncing that not only literature but human experience in toto consists of nothing except equivocal traces of arbitrary signs, they achieved self-interment. But a guild on the whole so adaptable may very well have a knack for sensing the future.

Some of the brighter critics are now teasing affirmative views of language out of early modern texts—from troubled masters, so to speak, rather than immune masters. In "The Question of Genius" (1986), Richard Poirier speculates:

> That, I think, is what Emerson means by the taut phrase "this riddle of liberty." He was ready to teach us, long before Foucault, that if we intend ever to resist our social and cultural fate, then we must first see it for what it is and that its form, ultimately, is the language we use in learning to know ourselves. Language is also, however, the place wherein we can most effectively register our dissent from fate. . . . Through such resistances, more than through directly political ones, sporadic evidence might emerge of some truer self or genius.

Robert Scholes's excellent book *Textual Power* (1985) is another harbinger of returning confidence. A few years ago the title might have signaled menace—the power of texts over us. Or it might have hinted at an analogy between texts and the black holes postulated by astronomers: a cluster of energy so dense it prevents light from escaping = an arrangement of symbols that refer only to themselves. As it is, Scholes in effect scorns to marvel or despair naively at the brute existence of the process of encoding, decoding, and recoding. Instead, he proposes that we use our linguistic powers critically to undo encoded acts of appropriation and domination.

Which way the wind is blowing, I hope. Whether Poirier has correctly decoded a particular passage by Emerson is a matter of scholarly judgment. However, the lesson of the great panic he stated very well in his own words. Language is the only way to get around the obstacle of language.

Reform from Below

It is of course legitimate to use *liberal* as a situational word, just as we use the word *tall*. A short adult is tall in comparison with a child, and a tall story is benign compared with a swindle. Although in the abstract an absolute monarchy would not seem to be the place to look for liberalism, surely A. J. Ayer is within his linguistic rights to say in his book on Voltaire that as regent for Louis XV, who succeeded to the throne at the age of five, Philippe d'Orléans "instituted a far more liberal regime" than Louis XIV had permitted. It was at least plausible for early advocates of laissez-faire capitalism to style their program liberal in contrast to certain narrowly held privileges under the old aristocratic order; as it was later plausible for early partisans of the welfare state to term themselves liberal in their contest with entrenched business interests. The left had real grounds on some occasions for regarding liberals as wishy-washy but well-meaning centrists who could be shoved in the proper direction, on other occasions as irredeemable technicians and window dressers for the rich and powerful. Correspondingly, the right had reason at times to view liberals as potentially dangerous heretics, at other times as a safe and compliant opposition.

Given this relativity and these historical flip-flops, it has been easy to make corrupt use of the word, polluting language in the process. An authoritarian regime, deciding to dump a particular class of dissenters abroad instead of paying for prison camps, may speak of its new and liberal emigration policy. George Bush in his 1988 campaign against Michael Dukakis probably calculated that the half of the population that votes contains a high percentage of those who think of themselves as good Americans but prize inequality. He managed simultaneously to disparage Dukakis by calling him a liberal and to make *liberal* a disparaging term by association with Dukakis.

Although they have nothing in common with *liberal* intrinsically, *reform* and *reformer, revolution* and *revolutionary* have been pulled into the same zone of slippery meaning. *Reformer* in John Calvin's time meant a person willing to kill and be killed in order to overthrow Europe's orthodox creed. Several generations later it could be applied matter-of-factly to someone petitioning for a reduction in tariffs. At first the revolutionary, an inspired/demented person (or process), staked everything on liberating/destroying society so as to create a brave new order/brutish tyranny. Eventually, in the fast and loose modern lexicon, the word came in handy for advertising and propaganda. A sale on pantyhose at the mall over Fourth of July weekend is revolutionary, and the glory of a slightly better than average potato crop belongs to the revolutionary cadre.

Postmodern doctrine holds that such words as *reform* and *revolution* have no meaning left. Upon passage by the Senate of legislation reducing the number of tax brackets (to raise approximately the same revenue), Ronald Reagan said to the press: "This is a great day for America. . . . The Senate bill is visionary in its scope and revolutionary in its implications." This indeed sounds meaningless. Perhaps an old ham paid to make tribal noises simply recited lines put in front of him. But we cannot afford to tune out, because important messages may be concealed in such utterances. In another context David Stockman, recounting his days as a budgeteer, warned against what he believed to be a deliberate Reaganite effort to cripple the United States government with debt and thus hinder social programs, which, if true, would certainly invest those lines with meaning. So long as we are still conscious (a matter postmoderns have not yet settled), the prudent course is to assign meaning to words, using current intelligence and historical reflection as a guide.

Under historical analysis one pattern of reference which emerges from the semantic haze is that interpretation of reform varies with the social credentials of the would-be reformer. Those customarily admitted to the policy process may go at each other hammer and tongs to advance or block a given reform, but the survivors are likely to maintain diplomatic relations. The law-abiding public may be pleased or irritated with the outcome, indifferent to it, scarcely aware of it, but not scandalized by the mere possibility of adjustment. Both insiders and social bystanders take a more excitable view, however, if reform is proposed by someone who is not supposed to make proposals. Whatever "uppity Nigras" and "the girls" said they wanted in the good old racist-sexist days was quickly skipped over, either in outrage because these low-status groups were making demands at all or (among sympathizers) in exultation because they had gathered the courage to demand anything.

This matter of social standing helps to explain why liberals of the sort who become college deans and broadcasting producers are so wedded to a vision of moderate change, openmindedness, responsible experimentation, and similar clichés. If they are allowed to tinker and agitate, it means they have the right credentials. Win or lose on a given issue, they are able to use the reformer's role as a career steppingstone and to enhance their self-esteem. They usually run no drastic personal risk even in a sharp contest, for the more intelligent movers and shakers understand that meliorism draws attention away from what actually goes on in corporations and bureaucracies. For the socially acceptable, at home with the procedures of incremental, legalistic politics, efforts at reform can be stimulating. They belong to the world where committees are formed, reports issued, budgets calculated, compromises reached, images engineered.

This is not to say that accredited reformers lack enemies. Ideologists of the right vehemently object that too much or the wrong kind of change has already been permitted, that hard-headed social discipline ought to be restored or strengthened in place of wishy-washy accommodation. Piece by piece, upstarts and subversives get through reformist trickery what they could not get in an open clash of principles and would not dare seek if they were dealt with firmly in the first place. Insofar as it is genuine, this view appears to be hopelessly wrong in identifying the agents of change. Some kinds of change the managerial class runs after, starting with subsidies for their enterprises. In the name of technology, economics, and institutional imperatives, they are perfectly willing to alter beyond recognition anything from a neighborhood to the climate of the earth.

Reform is despised by ideologists of the left too. It is seen as just so much tinkering to prolong a rotten social order, just a way of buying off dissent with token concessions. Sifting the American past from this point of view, the eye falls on such reformist episodes as the one climaxed by President Eisenhower when he ordered the lowest security classification for government documents abolished. The announced aim was to discourage secrecy in government and get rid of useless files. But the result was that the departments reclassified the bulk of their papers under other categories. The trouble with the leftish view is that it condescends to low-status people. Sometimes *they* initiate reform, with a goal in mind that means more than a mere concession to them, and *they* pay with their hides whether the reform is achieved or not.

Left, right, and center all discharge their conceptions into the semantic stream. Books and articles and editorials, interviews and public service advertisements, speeches and task force pronouncements flow from all sides. The word *reform* spins and bobs among a variety of other words—*compassion* one day, *productivity* another day, and so on. There is a sort of main channel, however, marked out in the textbooks. It runs along the following lines.

Social and political adjustments are desirable from time to time, and these can be made more efficiently and humanely without the burden of class conflict. Avoid the polarization of society. Plan, tune, but don't fix what's not broken. The creation of the Federal Reserve is a good example. No one was shot or exiled in curbing an erratic banking system, and yet market forces were still allowed plenty of play. As a result of the Federal Reserve, individual citizens are more secure in their personal finances, and the country in general is more stable and prosperous and thus better able to lead the Free World. Being responsible educators, we will mention in passing that some people think the stability is a precarious by-product of making the world safe for central banks. But let's not dwell on that. For a sobering example of turning to extremism rather than reform, look at the Civil War.

As already suggested, the textbook version omits the social status of the would-be reformer as an independent variable (and a rich source of sobering examples). If low-status people attempt reform, they are likely to be punished for trying and punished for success. The benefits of reform from below are likely to be appropriated at the top. In the case of reform as in many other things, life at the bottom is different as well as harder. Every institution, every social locale has a bottom level, and the people there are a low caste in that setting regardless of their status on some general scale. The empress is "only a woman."

The composite drawn by textbook writers is incomplete. Reform from below entails differences in rhetoric, action, and consequence. Five points representing a considerable amount of historical experience will make this clear.

1. The Snub

When Cesar Chavez began to organize Arizona farm workers in the spring of 1972, collective bargaining had been a well-known concept for over a century and a routine part of American life for roughly forty years. Not liked any better than taxes perhaps, but normal. "As far as I'm concerned," said Governor Jack Williams when he got wind of what the farm workers wanted, "these people don't exist." In 1964 when students at Berkeley sought freedom of speech, constitutional rights had been a prominent concept since the eighteenth century. At first, however, university administrators declared there could be no such issue on campus because their rules were "not negotiable." About that same time in Mississippi some black teenage boys told white police that they would use freedom to eat in restaurants and vote. Two policemen immediately clubbed one of the boys in the head.

Archetypal in this as in other ways, the Lawrence, Massachusetts, textile workers' strike of 1912 and events leading up to it offer a painful example of the snub. On January 1, 1912, a state law came into effect which reduced the maximum number of hours women and children might be employed from fifty-six hours per week to fifty-four hours per week. (A triumph of reform from above!) At that time the wool manufacturers had enjoyed tariff protection for half a century. Simultaneously through immigration they were able to work their mills with the equivalent of the cheap foreign labor they supposedly deserved protection against. About 85 percent of the thirty thousand Lawrence textile workers were unskilled and nonunionized. Furthermore they were divided among themselves by ethnic friction —for there were British, French, Belgian, Polish, Italian, Lithuanian, and other groups. The majority of workers in the woolen mills were women and children paid by the hour. On the one hand the slight reduction in hours did little to relieve fatigue. If anything it encouraged employers to speed up the work when they had an abundance of orders, so as to get the same output from the shorter, cheaper schedule. On the other hand these women and children (and the men in their families) lived close enough to subsistence that the reduction in income hurt. Some of the bolder workers asked for a wage increase equal to their loss. Others simply asked for an exemption allowing them to work two more hours. In their curt refusal the mill owners assumed that workers were entitled to a reply but not an explanation.

2. Rub Their Noses in It

If, despite being denied permission to exist, low-status reformers succeed in publicizing a grievance, a common response is to proudly confirm inequity and reinforce it as the way things should be. Once again the experience of Arizona farm workers is illuminating. When Chavez pressed on with his organizing, the state's lawmakers had to reckon with the fact that Arizona belonged to a society in which picketing, striking, and boycotting were legitimate under designated rules and that the organizers might play the dirty trick of complying with the rules. Their answer was to pass a law prohibiting specifically farm workers from engaging in these activities. The principle was nothing new. Back in the first half of the nineteenth century, the Society of Saint Tammany in New York City normally sounded out its supporters in nominating candidates for public office. On one occasion a group of Irish-American tradesmen and laborers raised a point of equity. Since they supported the society, they reasoned, the society ought to include someone from their group on the slate of men standing for election. The initial reaction was to exclude anyone with an Irish name. When that brought on a boisterous protest, the Tammany caucus called in tavern rowdies to beat up the troublemakers and throw them out of the meeting hall.

3. *Good Behavior Is Wicked*

The presentation of demands in a legally and socially correct manner by someone from the wrong side of the tracks is deemed to be offensive and subversive if not criminal. The first approach of the Lawrence woolen workers mentioned above—hesitant, awkward, amateurish—met a simple refusal. But when IWW organizers Joseph J. Ettor and Arturo Giovannitti arrived on the scene, formed a businesslike strike committee representing all ethnic and craft groupings, boiled down complaints and hard feelings to five definite demands, and proposed negotiations to the employers, the going got rough. The two Wobblies were soon arrested on charges of being accessory to murder and held without bail. Hundreds of other arrests on various pretexts followed. After the strikers won a pay increase, indirectly raising textile wages throughout New England for a time, the liberal magazine *Survey* could not forgive the insolence of creating a proper bargaining apparatus. "Are we to expect," the editors asked in the issue of April 6, 1912, "that instead of playing the game respectably [that is, humbly], or else frankly breaking out into lawless riots which we know well enough how to deal with, the laborers are to listen to a subtle anarchistic philosophy which challenges the fundamental idea of law and order . . . ?"

Of course response to reformers from below is most likely to turn vicious when a tangible interest is at stake, but a ferocious attitude toward "pretensions" lies near the surface at all times. For many years in the South, for example, if no particular fault could be found with a solvent, literate, neatly dressed black man going about his business—rarity that he was—he might be addressed by whites as "professor," the same tag applied to whorehouse piano players. Similarly, feminist arguments for equal pay, solidly constructed around economic and legal data, triggered contemptuous remarks in the 1970s about "women and cripples."

Since a demonstration by the "wrong element" that they are

capable of acting properly within the system in which they seek to be included frightens and angers those already inside, it follows that the more comprehensive and convincing the demonstration of fitting in, the more extreme the denial. The so-called Dorr War in Rhode Island in the 1840s was a classic episode. Thomas Wilson Dorr and his fellow suffragists had to create a duplicate government in order to vote.

The issues that Dorr and other suffragists brought to a head in 1842 stemmed from the fact that Rhode Island alone among the states had no constitution. The basic law was still the charter granted by Charles II in 1663.

The grievances felt most keenly under this outmoded charter were four. First, an archaic definition of property requirements barred about half the adult white males in Rhode Island from voting. Dorr himself, who had served as a bank commissioner and a member of the Providence School Committee, was not allowed to vote. Second, communities where newer forms of wealth and trade flourished were underrepresented in the state's legislative assembly. Newport, for instance, though it had long since fallen behind Providence in population and business activity, still sent more representatives to the General Assembly than any other town. Third, charter government authorized the governor, his deputy, and ten elected assistants to sit in the assembly (they held a seventh of the seats), and judges were appointed by the assembly at will. Fourth, to petitions at various times during the preceding fifty years for a referendum, for a constitutional convention, and for statutory change, the enfranchised "freemen" invariably responded by heaping scorn on the suffragists for their presumption.

This scorn could hardly have been more provocative to the suffragists of Dorr's generation, for they prided themselves on their fitness to operate in a "true American" political system if admitted. In the fall of 1841 a state suffrage committee and a host of delegates from local suffrage associations framed a People's Constitution, whose adoption by a majority of Rhode Island citizens, they proclaimed, ought to override the obsolete government of the state. On December 27, in apparently honest balloting at town and ward polls set up by suffrage associations outside the law, 13,944 votes were cast in favor of adopting the People's Constitution, and almost none were cast against (those opposed stayed away from this shadow election).

In the spring of 1842 Dorr, long a prominent suffragist, ran for governor under the People's Constitution in balloting organized in the same way. He, about a hundred People's Assemblymen, and four candidates for lesser executive offices were elected by more than six thousand votes. On May 3 they held an inauguration in Providence and created their own militia. The People's Assembly rapidly passed a number of reforms and adjourned.

Meanwhile Samuel Ward King, the law-and-order candidate, had been elected governor by a vote of 4,864 to 2,211 under the old charter. On May 4 the charterist government-elect met at Newport and declared a state of insurrection.

Approximately 180 Dorrites (officials and electoral clerks) were now liable to arrest. About half a dozen arrests were in fact made by charter agents during the first few days of Dorrite government, and a dozen or so Dorrite officials resigned in the same interval. The speeches issuing from Providence began to hint that the people's government might yield in return for reforms.

Dorr, however, shortly acquired an outside ally. Wishing to appear as the champion of states' rights for reasons of their own, Tammany politicians in New York entertained Dorr, staged mass meetings in his honor, and made belligerent speeches in support of the "free people" of Rhode Island.

Although the New Yorkers probably wished to do no more than embarrass the current federal administration, which reluctantly supported the charterists, Dorr took heart and sent out his militia to capture the principal armory in the Providence area. An overly complicated plan of attack failed when their cannon misfired. Eleven more Dorrite assemblymen resigned. Most of the other suffragist officers went into hiding or were arrested.

Late in June Dorr and twenty New Yorkers linked up with about two hundred volunteer riflemen at the village of Chepachet, Rhode Island. The Dorr War now looked fierce indeed, for the rebels took up a fortified hill position to await the charter troops marching upon them. But on the day of battle not a single shot troubled the birds nesting on Acote's Hill. Greatly outnumbered, the Dorrites surrendered, hid, or ran. Dorr himself scurried over the New York border.

4. Success Must Be Punished

Broadening the franchise and modernizing state government proved to be easily arranged after all. By the fall of 1843 the authorities had a new Rhode Island constitution in place. First things first, however. Between June 26 and August 28 after the rout at Chepachet, about 350 suffragists were hauled in and abused with no prosecution intended. In one case, for example, sixteen people were held for several days in a nine-by-twelve cell. Several hundred others had their belongings thrown about and trampled in the course of "searches" by charterist agents. Dorr, who returned to Providence on October 31, 1843, expecting amnesty, was sentenced to life imprisonment at hard labor (a sentence commuted in 1845 after his health had been permanently ruined).

In effect he was punished for insubordination, a perennial risk for reformers from below, seen many times before and after poor Dorr. A similar pattern of acceptance and vindictiveness was evident at Berkeley in the 1960s. By the end of January 1965 the changes for which the Free Speech Movement had fought were adopted as official university policy, and FSM voluntarily disbanded. Months later, nevertheless, thirty students were sent to prison for their participation in the Sproul Hall sit-in the year before. The California legislature cut the budget for teaching assistants. President Clark Kerr persuaded the regents to exclude graduate students from student government. Chancellor Martin Meyerson expelled a former FSM leader for obscenity.

Perhaps the most instructive episode of this sort in American history took place in colonial North Carolina. There wealthy men of affairs in the eastern half of the colony managed to alienate the western half from representative government before the American Revolution had even begun. The War of the Regulators was a classic case of crushing reformers while meeting their demands.

During the late 1760s, a time when colonial administrators appointed by the crown considered themselves entitled to make money from their office, one William Tryon was named governor of North Carolina and rapidly aligned himself with the eastern oligarchs. Under

Tryon two kinds of government agents gained office in the western settlements. There were "gentlemen" whose loyalties and ambitions pointed eastward. And there were toughs and spoilsmen who carried out tax collecting and court business in the spirit of bandits (keeping about half the receipts for themselves, as Tryon admitted). Each time a document was attested, a deed transferred, a claim litigated—common acts in a yeoman community under Anglo-American law—court officers and court-appointed attorneys collected extortionate fees (as much as five times higher than the officially prescribed amount).

Beginning about 1765 the men of six frontier counties petitioned the governor and the assembly for relief from this extortion. When the petitions were ignored, a so-called Regulation movement was organized to try the ballot. Regulators from four counties succeeded in getting elected to the assembly in 1769, but Tryon quickly dissolved the body and procured a new one which gave him a stronger riot act. The Regulators also demanded prosecution of corrupt officers in 1768 and 1769. A few officials were convicted of charging excessive fees, but the victory was hollow. While the most notorious exploiter of offices scratched up his fine of "one penny and cost," three Regulator leaders were condemned for "incitement to rebellion" and saved from hanging only by a humiliating pardon.

As a result of such treatment, Regulator threats and angry rallies multiplied in 1770. Killings, beatings, tax refusals, and forcible disruptions of the courts occurred. By 1771 the Regulators brought taxation, law enforcement, and court proceedings to a standstill in the back country. They declared certain government agents to be outlaws. They moved about the countryside menacingly in armed groups.

Tryon responded by calling out the militia in 1771. His force of about fourteen hundred militiamen, of whom over a thousand were easterners, marched west to restore order and, if possible, to draw the Regulators into a pitched battle. On May 16 a force of Regulators somewhat larger than the governor's army made a stand at Alamance Creek. Casualties in the ensuing two-hour battle were nearly equal: nine men killed on each side and several score wounded. The governor's troops won decisively, however, in the sense of scattering or capturing the entire Regulator force.

In the aftermath, seven Regulators were executed, and about sixty were outlawed (most of whom fled the colony). Tryon imposed a spiteful loyalty oath on the rest as a condition of pardon.

Thus the Regulator movement was broken, but the punishment of upstarts was no obstacle to appropriating reforms they conceived. Less than a year after the Battle of Alamance, the assembly tightened the law for appointing sheriffs, revised and restricted court fees, and increased western representation by creating four new counties.

5. Appropriations

Most chiefs would like to be both feared and loved by their Indians. So if a gang of nobodies create an uproar over reform, reactions such as those described above are elementary for anyone in authority at the time. Get in the last blow. Since it falls on upstarts who are no longer so strident, having made their point as best they could at loss to themselves, punitive action now takes on the dignity of judgment rather than brawling. Save face by "granting" what has to be accepted anyway to soothe public uneasiness aroused by the reformers. In Rhode Island the charterist regime that crushed Dorr installed a modern constitution, reapportioned representation to reflect population changes, and specified limits on the use of martial law. At Berkeley a faculty Select Committee on Education glossed the recent confrontations over with phrases such as "introducing experimentation" on campus. Chancellor Roger Heyns, who replaced Martin Meyerson, spoke sanctimoniously of "restoring community."

Adroit operators do not stop there, however. Those who continue in authority, as well as subchiefs, future chiefs, and chiefs from the other side of the mountain, see the new status quo not as the conclusion of a reform episode but as a lever like any other which may be to their advantage to grasp. Alabama Congressman Oscar W. Underwood, for example, chairman of the House Ways and Means Committee, exploited the publicity the IWW had given to high profits in the woolen industry during the Lawrence strike. He managed on the one hand to please the cotton interests in his home territory and on the other hand to enter the history books as a progressive by cosponsoring the Underwood-Simmons Tariff of 1913, which lowered the import duty on woolens. In 1934 militia and vigilantes smashed a national textile strike and the San Francisco general strike. In 1937 Republic Steel garrisoned its South Chicago plant with police who sallied out for open warfare with workers in the neighborhood, wounding several. Such events were important in producing the Fair Labor Standards Act of 1938. This law, which was in many ways a mopping up after a bloody mess in a time of crisis unforeseen a few years earlier, Franklin Roosevelt chose to call "far-sighted"—a clever stroke no matter how interpreted.

In short, it is common for chiefs to appropriate reforms that originate below. In North Carolina westerners did not find the reforms conceived by the Regulators much help when administered by their enemies. Roughly fifteen hundred people from the back counties moved to the future state of Tennessee within three years after the Battle of Alamance. Those who remained in Regulator country tended to stay out of the American Revolution, less because they opposed independence than because the eastern establishment occupied the important military and civil posts. Samuel Johnston, author of the riot act that had pleased the royal governor, became president of the Provincial Congress in 1775. The colonels of the first two North Carolina regiments mustered for revolutionary service had made their reputation as anti-Regulators.

Trying to police word usage is as futile as trying to enforce sumptuary laws. Foucault and his followers, obsessed with class bias and arbitrary but inescapable rules of syntax, portray language as a prison. They could as easily fret about looseness as rigidity. In truth language is like a net with large rips and tangles. *Unravel*, a classic example in English, became the synonym for *ravel*. After a thousand years as a gender-neutral adjective meaning merry and high-spirited, *gay* changes into a mood-neutral label for male homosexuals. The word is then used so rarely in any but the new sense that future historians might assume the traditional meaning was quickly forgotten, except that fluent speakers obviously remember the old meaning because they distinguish *gaiety* from *gayness*. By the year 2000, to give one more example, it probably will be forgotten that *could care less* was originally expressed as *could not care less*. People talk. Language drifts.

For sure, precision in language is not a universal concern. If the aspects of reform analyzed in this essay were explained on the back of cereal boxes and TV program guides, that would not necessarily make anyone more scrupulous in using the word. Thanks to the fluidity of the linguistic universe, however, there is room in the world even for a minority to whom conscientious speech matters.

At a minimum, conscientiousness with regard to *reform* means avoiding and rejecting two false assumptions. Contrary to much loose speech, reform is not generically—sometimes not even relatively—a painless way to make a change. Nor is it a homogenous experience whose social point of origin in any given case is merely circumstantial.

There is a phrase, the Age of Reform, which refers to the period at the end of the nineteenth century and the beginning of the twentieth century in America. It is understood among the sophisticated that such rubrics, which can't possibly represent all that happens in an era, come and go according to what in the past holds interest in the present. By all means let us be sophisticated. During the Age of Reform, between 1889 and 1918, over twenty-five hundred black people were lynched in the United States.

Fenimore Cooper
and the Invention of Writing

Marxism, Thorstein Veblen used to say, is too logical. Not that he had anything against logic. He was strongly attracted to it himself. But doctrinal thinking could not in his judgment capture the incoherence of American life.

The Founding Fathers, for example, broke off from England to preserve their rights as Englishmen! In the Declaration of Independence they expressed a desire to abide by tradition and British constitutional practices—a desire thwarted, according to them, only because of radical and illegitimate changes introduced by King George and his evil ministers. Proceeding to win a revolutionary war without much political theory behind it, they then had to create a government. The one they made on the second try was, and as governments go still is, a good one. Its virtues were functional, however, virtues akin to those of well-designed modular furniture that can be rearranged or even converted to new purposes as times change. Again not much doctrine.

These men must have expected writers to appear in the country they created. Most of them had been exposed to theological writings supported by Scripture. Most of them were lawyers or had transacted business through charters, deeds, contracts, and other legal texts. There were plans afoot for additional universities, learned societies, and outlets for scientific papers. Most of them were familiar with pamphleteering and partisan newspapers, and they had considered the place of the press in the republic they were constructing. Some of them were at home with classical authors and British and French literature and thus used to the idea of the literary artist. One day, presumably, more Americans would turn out odes, dramas, memoirs, and so forth. Yet in discussing social roles proper to the new country they said little about writers as such. No social place was provided for the professional writer. The declaration of literary independence was left to the next generation.

The person who took the lead in this mission was James Fenimore Cooper (1789–1851), who became for a time one of the best known and most widely translated writers in the world: the author not only of frontier tales and sea stories but also of social novels, travel books, naval histories, and disquisitions on politics—forty-two volumes in all and a host of pieces for magazines and newspapers. He called explicitly for "mental independence" from Britain and insisted that genuine literature could and should be made from American material in an American style. Furthermore his victories as a plaintiff influenced the development of American libel law and the rights of the press under the First Amendment. He was a pillar of society as well, a man who went to school with Livingstons, Jays, and Van Rensselaers, became chummy with Lafayette and other Europeans of the "better sort," and fulfilled patrician obligations by serving in such offices as chairman of the local Bible Society. The cream of the American literary community that grew up in his time—Emerson, Longfellow, Hawthorne, Melville, Parkman—attended or sent tributes to be read at memorial services upon his death.

True to the pattern of the burgeoning American culture which he did so much to advance, Cooper wove many discrepancies and inconsistencies into his accomplishments, more even than the colonials of his father's generation who had backed into a successful revolution. For one thing he was clumsy with words and improved very little with practice. "Neither the gondolier nor the mariner of Calabria spoke until their riveted gazes after the retiring figure became useless" is a representative sentence from *The Bravo*, a book written well along in Cooper's career. "The great difficulty . . . in suddenly overcoming the *vis inertiae* of so large a mass" was his idea of an exciting way to narrate a hairbreadth escape by boat from a scalping party in *The Deerslayer*. Routinely he padded his books, as when he used seven hundred words to inform the reader that summers are warm and trees cast shade. He wrote awful dialogue, as in: "Thy case is piteous, Jacopo! Thou hast need of ghostly counsel." He wobbled between romance and realistic action, poesy and verisimilitude. "Cooper," wrote Mark Twain in a rollicking retrospective essay around 1900, "has scored 114 offences against literary art out of a possible 115. It breaks the record. . . . When a personage talks like an illustrated, gilt-edged, tree-calf, hand-tooled, seven-dollar Friendship's Offering in the beginning of a paragraph, he shall not talk like a negro minstrel in the end of it. But this rule is flung down and danced upon in the *Deerslayer* tale." Twain went on to ridicule Cooper's operatic scenes of tracking, ambushes, and marksmanship (especially one in which Natty Bumppo borrows a stranger's rifle and drills a target that is, if you make the calculation, too far away to be visible).

The discrepancy between how much Cooper wrote and how awkwardly he wrote was nothing, though, compared with his fitful sense of what would interest readers. Whereas some of his books sold barely enough copies to pay the printer's bill, in the Leatherstocking Tales he lit up the national psyche and fascinated readers around the world. He was the author above all others who put the snapping twig, the war whoop, and the invincible rifleman into literature. In effect he invented the Western, not only its action and suspense components but also the chaste love interest, the pathos of the Vanishing Redman, and the ambivalence about the taming of the wilderness. No wonder writers came to his funeral. He had pioneered a symbol trade analogous to the fur trade, by which frontier life was processed into a popular literary commodity for sale in the cities.

It would be nice to believe that Cooper sifted sensitively through the history of many native peoples until he settled on the Mohicans for his example of tragic conflict between red and white. At a time when they and their neighbors were still relatively strong in combination, the southern Mohicans quarreled with the Pequots, who, left on their own, were soon overrun by white colonists. Then at ultimately high cost to themselves the Mohicans joined as mercenaries in the struggle between France and England for North America. Finally they ceded their home territory to the newly independent Americans and settled on a little reservation in Connecticut, where disease, hunger, and social collapse finished them off around 1800. Yet Cooper may have chosen to write about the Mohicans simply because legends and fragments of history concerning them happened to be known in the part of New York state where he had a home. Worse, he may have found it convenient to wax sentimental over a people who could no longer be helped. He apparently was not curious about the equally sad story of the northern branch (of what is properly called the Mahican group) and in any case did not live to see the end of it. Under attack by the Iroquois, the northern Mohicans moved west to join the Delaware and soon lost their separate cultural identity. The Delaware thus "augmented" were in turn ruined. Those who embraced nonviolence under the influence of Moravian missionaries were massacred by frontiersmen in Pennsylvania. Those who drifted into the Ohio Valley fought on the losing side of several frontier wars and were dumped across the Mississippi. Used as Army scouts against the Plains tribes at little profit to themselves ("wolves for the blue soldiers"), they wound up in Oklahoma as a tiny, demoralized remnant.

There could hardly be a better illustration of Veblen's judgment about the incoherence of American culture than the ups and downs of Cooper's reputation after he died. At virtually the same moment that the likes of Emerson and Melville commemorated him for declaring national literary independence, another sort of eminent American transformed him into the genteel author of wholesome teacher-and-preacher-approved tales for juveniles. Of Daniel Webster Cooper had said "not a great man—merely a man of great peculiarities." Who should turn up at a memorial service in February 1852 but Webster. In a fulsome speech the great man praised the departed for "enlightening the rising generation without injury to their morals or any solicitation of depraved passions." Here was Cooper's reward for writing forty-two books and balancing on the tightwire of celebrity—to be complimented for not molesting children. And this peculiar reward came not just from Webster. A sizable number of readers adopted this view, so that well-meaning uncles went on giving *The Deerslayer* to youngsters for Christmas in that spirit right down to 1930 or so. Surely it was goody-goodyness that drew Mark Twain's fire more than Cooper himself, and he overlooked a development more dubious yet. All the while Cooper was pigeonholed as a safe writer for properly supervised youth, hacks and journeyman authors were borrowing from him, stealing from him, and upon his legacy building a mountain of thrillers, buckskin melodramas, and horse operas whose main appeal lay in violent action and lethal encounters. That violence depicted for profit should be deemed appropriate entertainment for the young is one of the abiding mysteries of America.

By 1930 confusion over Cooper (literary confusion at least) seemed to be giving way to common sense. Without claiming undue skill or profundity for him and without worrying about youthful "depravity," H. L. Mencken and Edmund Wilson alluded to him politely as a forerunner of better things and let it go at that. D. H. Lawrence included a chapter on Cooper in *Studies in Classic American Literature* and produced a resounding line: "The essential American soul is hard, isolate, stoic, and a killer." Lawrence nevertheless kept a sense of proportion about Cooper's yarns. "Of course it never rains: it is never cold and muddy and dreary: no one has wet feet or toothache: no one ever feels filthy when they can't wash for a week."

Just when it appeared that he would be permitted to rest in honorable retirement, more posthumous bad luck cropped up for Cooper. The Age of Criticism arrived. For the next twenty or so years modernist critics fought for control of English departments and influence in the press with the aim of substituting their methods and values for what they regarded as the shallow appreciation and genteel antiquarianism of earlier critics and scholars. As with any expanding profession, output had to be assured, busywork found, career niches carved. There was room for only a few full-time Cooper specialists, but any critic might get a chapter or an article out of the unread books or use Cooper as a springboard from which to launch an interpretation of American culture (by the 1950s elevated to American "civilization"). Vernon Parrington, Lionel Trilling, Philip Rahv, and Quentin Anderson took a look at Cooper in passing. Collectively quite a bit was done in the period from Robert E. Spiller's *Fenimore Cooper: Critic of His Times* (1931) to John P. McWilliams's *Political Justice in a Republic: James Fenimore Cooper's America* (1972). Documented biographies were written; comprehensive bibliographies were compiled; annotated journals and letters were published. Cooper's artistry and ideas were analyzed far beyond the thought he had given to them. He figured in several thematic books such as Henry Nash Smith's *Virgin Land* and Leslie Fiedler's *Love and Death in the American Novel*.

A double discrepancy this time. The campaign to rehabilitate Cooper made less critical sense than the let-well-enough-alone view it supplanted and failed to induce the public to read the Cooper whom it purported to make more knowable than ever before. Like a business conglomerate that rushes to buy whatever property can be had, the academicians took Cooper over without considering whether they could do him any good.

Some members of the new critical establishment tried diplomacy as a means of restoring Cooper to favor. Yvor Winters in *Maule's Curse*, for example, attempted to make Cooper's occasionally skillful renderings of scene and character appear strong by contrasting them with priggish, awkward, florid passages. In *James Fenimore Cooper* Donald Ringe said: "Once we learn to accept the old-fashioned and sometimes careless style, we can appreciate Cooper's fundamental artistry." Vernon Parrington equated Cooper's alleged boldness in speaking his mind "unterrified by public opinion" with artistic and intellectual substance—a dubious jump in logic to begin with and especially precarious in the case of a writer who was shocked by the racy talk of Parisian women at the dinner table.

Other critics in effect praised their man for his chauvinism. Thus in *The Eccentric Design* Marius Bewley called *The Deerslayer* "one of the most important masterpieces of American literature," implying a national stock of masterpieces so abundant that the reader's only problem was to avoid wasting time on negligible ones. The United States, Cooper had asserted in 1828, was tops in "everything that constitutes general moral superiority." Surely material superiority must follow as the natural award. "Every man sees and feels," he wrote in 1850, "that a state is rapidly advancing to maturity which must reduce the pretensions of even ancient Rome to supremacy to a secondary place in the estimation of mankind." Regarding a native son who saw the light so early and whose sentiments were so darn right, it was a pleasure to cite his firsts and near firsts. In a 1952 article Howard Mumford Jones listed nine firsts in a single paragraph (first American novelist of the sea, et cetera). A tireless researcher reported that Ostego Hall, built by Cooper's father, boasted the first avenue of Lombardy poplars in the United States. Cooper was even identified as one of the first true Americans in his dislike of cities. "An undue proportion of the dissolute, unsettled, vicious, and disorganizing collect in towns," he had declared.

Critics to whom chauvinism and writing-well-in-fragments did not appeal chose yet a different strategy of rehabilitation. They categorized Cooper as a social theorist who happened to write mostly in the form of tales and polemics. This gave them license to go through all the novels again, extracting the author's "ideas" from the fiction in which they were embedded. At the same time this brought Cooper's nonfiction books, articles, letters, and public addresses firmly under their jurisdiction.

Alas, the social-theorist strategy fizzled too. Robert Spiller set a poor example at the beginning with an obtuse sense of social reality. Describing Cooper's wedding day, for instance, he tossed in the following speculation: "The jolly black Mammie—then probably enjoying the idyllic security of slavery—bustled about the kitchen preparing the wedding supper." Even Cooper a hundred years earlier, though he conceived of racial characteristics as absolutely fixed, had done better than this. He attributed separate worthy "gifts" (a favorite word) to reds, blacks, and whites. Forty years after Spiller, John P. McWilliams in a prolix book applauded the novelist for "moral courage" for asserting "that a republic that cannot combine political equality with inequality of condition was doomed to failure." To tell the truth, this "idea" was one of a set of contradictory opinions held by a well-off white male who in his final book, *The Ways of the Hour*, denigrated the Married Women's Property Act and thus opposed any kind of equality for half the population. In 1832 in a letter to Horace Greenough he complained that Americans had greater "reverence for fraud and selfishness than for anything else." At other times, however, both before and after, he maintained that the American upper class was the bedrock of decency. Cooper's social ideas did not develop or cohere. They simply fluctuated and over the long run ran a haphazard life course.

Since it is too late to heed Mencken and Wilson by leaving well enough alone, what use can we find for Cooper and how can we make it up to him for the misguided attentions of prudes and academicians? Passé and antiquated he may be, but he is our aboriginal famous writer.

There lies the clue. We know the perils of the role, memorably expressed in a recent article by Alison Lurie:

> The American reading public prefers famous writers to suffer. The approved pattern is a meteoric rise like that of a Roman candle, exploding into brilliance at its apogee and then descending and becoming extinguished in the glare of newer fountains of colored fire. The descent ideally will be haunted by demons of a particularly nasty sort and end in a classical purgation of terror and fear, with biographers and critics scrambling round to pick up the holy cinders.

Cooper deserves credit for running the gauntlet first. In a country then even less prepared for writers and thus in a role he was compelled to make up as he went along, his powers of improvisation were remarkable. Poe added the element of self-destruction through alcohol and sexual fiascoes, and Melville supplied the agony of the has-been. Otherwise the role of the writer in America remains much as Cooper created it 150 years ago. It is still the role that first novelists reviewed in next Sunday's *New York Times* will be stepping into.

Random self-selection is the first characteristic in the pattern that Cooper initiated. Individuals simply declare themselves to be writers. The proliferation of fiction workshops, poetry readings, and talk-show pundits has not altered the pattern essentially. Stephanie Dahl, a teacher of writing, recently recounted how she was stopped in the campus parking lot by a stranger who pressed her for advice on where to get his book published but refused to tell her what the book was about. "I try to remember that this is America," she said in good humor, "that dreams of bestsellerdom emanate from Horatio Alger, and that belief in the unique value of one's own life and work is inherent in the American character." She could have substituted Cooper for Alger's fictitious little hustlers. His qualifications for the literary life consisted of a pampered childhood, expulsion from Yale for roughing up a tutor, knocking around at sea, and wooing a Tory heiress. He is said to have written his first book as a lark, to show his wife that he could outdo a boring English novel they had read together. The story may be apocryphal and is almost certainly incomplete. Yet as a parable of the social isolation in which American writers begin and as an example of what passes for a public justification of the calling it rings true.

A great deal is customarily made by the self-chosen individuals of the solitude, alienation, and punishing loneliness they endure on account of their vocation. Yet they are in fact conforming with special zeal to a cultural imperative in favor of isolated achievement. Brian Sutton-Smith, an acute analyst of childhood, recently pointed out that American children play more with toys and less with each other than children do elsewhere. Toys are given to them by conscientious parents in effect to train them for individual activity. As George C. Scott protested, even acting, an ensemble profession, is transformed into a contest via the Academy Awards.

At some level would-be writers count on success in return for extreme devotion to cultural duty. If success comes, it does not necessarily reconcile them to the social order on the surface or even to the human race, which may remain the target of their work ad infinitum; but it makes them optimistic about the efficacy of individual talent. Although as a well-connected rich man's son Cooper always felt entitled to wealth and position, his complacency ballooned when his second novel made a splash. "If the laborer is indispensable to civilization, so also is the gentleman. While the one produces, the other directs his skill to those arts which raise the polished man above the barbarian," he said in *The American Democrat*. Politics need not intrude on "any of the principal interests of life." Settlement of the American wilderness combined the benefits of culture and nature without the drawbacks of either. Conflict over states' rights would dissolve painlessly, he thought, in a spirit of national loyalty.

When news of success spreads round the country, it gives writers a platform—an invitation to moral confusion and misuse of talent. Without a platform it might seem to them a waste of time to articulate opinions about subjects on which they have nothing useful to say and make gestures because they feel good. With a platform they are tempted to say whatever pops into their heads. Cooper, for instance, at heart a hereditary Federalist, gained little and contributed little by dipping into trendy concerns such as spiritualism and hypnotism as he grew older. Indeed, a platform wearied him while it gratified him. Like so many American writers to come, he sought relief from ratiocination through anti-intellectualism. In *Notions of the Americans* he pictured "lost in a maze of theories" as a hellish place to be and dismissed laws that "harmonize with other parts of an elaborate theory" in favor of those "intended to make men comfortable and happy." A platform, moreover, is a dubious location from which to carry on experiments in self-definition. Little personal codes take on too much importance. Never to drink beer from a glass, always from a can, might be an example of bohemian priggishness. Cooper, a genteel prig, took pride with Mrs. Cooper in the fact that their children "did not need a hint" that they should decline invitations to parties held on Sundays. Writers who issue manifestos and turn out for demonstrations decade after decade—always championing up-to-date causes, sometimes suffering for them—are often more interested in the right attitude than in the right formula for money, votes, organization, bargaining tactics, weapons, or whatever would advance the cause in the long run. It takes a knack for self-absorption to examine one's conscience in a crowd.

When publication and publicity are guaranteed in advance by past success, writers tend to overestimate the loyalty of vendors and readers to the self formed and the work offered. Whether the initial success came through luck, merchandising, or merit is a detail to the public. Whether the successful book was cute, trashy, profound, controversial, sentimental, or whatever does not matter all that much. The world is full of cute, profound, et cetera books. What's exciting in a commodity culture is that someone passed the market test with flying colors. The "growth" of a writer means next to nothing if that specific excitement is not sustained. Correspondingly, writers tend to overlook the fact that readers operate in the same culture of self-pursuits as themselves. Writers presume that whatever occurs to them next ought to be written up and received with interest—critically perhaps but with a sense of continuity. When Cooper glorified America in fiction and told his countrymen in polemics that they were superior to foreigners, he was conscious of forming the ideas, of composition, of presentation. That they might be absorbed in their own concerns and barely aware of his performance carried little weight with him. Upon his initial success as a spinner of frontier adventures he went abroad, discovered a variety of landscapes and the intricacy of European society, and "reported." It amazed and hurt him that many readers did not care about his growing knowledge or share his changing interests. Only a few of them disputed his message that the Catskills were less majestic than the Alps and that American breakfasts were greasy. They simply decided what they liked to read as unilaterally as he decided what he wanted to write—and shunned his new books.

Time on the platform and the problem of what to do for an encore generally hardens writers. In middle life, as would be the case with many successors, Cooper became more embroiled, more observant, and more calculating. He noticed that pioneers could be feckless and destructive as well as heroic and that "progress" entails costs as well as benefits. In campaigning for international copyright protection and in lawsuits against the Whig press he knowingly pursued personal advantage. He agonized egotistically over the loss of readers.

To his credit, Cooper first responded to the problem of lost readers by trying to become a better writer—broadening his range, trying to see deeper into life. Drawing on gumption he had not used for a while and recognizing literary ideals he had not admitted before, he turned from "mere action" to more complicated characters, more ambitious forms, and weightier themes. In this as in other ways he blazed a trail for American writers. Unfortunately, however, his novels of "purpose" bored the public even more than the travel books. His audience shrank to less than half the size it had been, and the disappointment stopped him in his tracks. He quit writing fiction for several years.

Toward the middle of the 1840s Cooper tried the other trail that many writers in his predicament have since followed. To make money, he returned to his old adventure formulas and in fact regained popularity. Though perhaps he took a craftsman's pride by that time in the skill with which he readjusted the ratio of entertainment to purpose, the experience cannot have felt good. With old age came a sour conservatism expressed directly in his nonfiction. Sanctity of contract more or less replaced republican virtue in his eyes as the best that could be expected in public affairs. He took a bitter satisfaction in pointing out how easily public opinion was manipulated, and he cackled over the dominance of big business that he foresaw—the sway of organized money that in fact came to pass in the age of robber barons a generation after his death.

That our founding novelist was known for writing about the frontier is certainly appropriate. The American expectation is still that writers will head out alone like trappers into the woods and some day return, if they don't get killed, with a bundle of pages for trading with a book club or a film producer. Closing the frontier has a nasty sound to Americans. Freedom to them borders on no permanent involvement, and in their fantasies at least they would rather face grizzly bears and Shawnee war parties than the terrors of collectivity.

This is not such a bad choice if the alternative is a society in which writers regard thought as onerous and statesmen associate literature with debauching children. Considering that 150 years have passed since Cooper's heyday, however, "frontiersman" is a meager and ramshackle role for writers. Far more than in his time we want writers, we expect writers, we have writers; but we continue to position them haphazardly on the organizational chart.

Though his skill at improvising can be admired, the pattern that Cooper pioneered is not the valuable part of his legacy. Rather, the persistence of that pattern holds a lesson. Just as they are inclined to think the past does not count, so Americans envision culture purely as a matter of choice, like ordering chocolate ice cream or vanilla ice cream. Terms such as *lifestyle* and *personal growth* imply that culture can be individualized and rearranged at will. For counterbalance we could use some expressions at the other extreme: perhaps "Children are fossils embedded already in a language and a common fate" or "Progress depends on survival." Yet here we are, circa 1990, doing things as they were done by a man who made it up as he went along five generations ago and is now virtually forgotten. Who knows what else looks natural and open only because our traditional way of looking at things determines what we see?

The Village Apollo

When Thoreau graduated from Harvard College in 1837, something was already amiss. His mother called him David. He preferred Henry. Ostensibly a believer in the cardinal American virtue of independence, she thought perhaps he should leave home to make his mark in the world. He broke into tears and stayed put.

Whether on balance it helped her to keep this sturdy but weepy fellow on the premises is hard to say. He was probably a competent handyman, because later he did odd jobs around Concord. Once, though, when she wanted him to spade the garden, he said that the death of his brother four months earlier had made him "too nervous." The bulk of handyman commissions, moreover, came from his famous friend Emerson and may have had more to do with patronage and kindness than with demand for his services. How many Harvard graduates end up as handymen anyway? And how many are both fanatically fond of books and too poor to acquire them? A few years later Thoreau the paragon of independence wrote an unctuous, wheedling letter to the president of Harvard, angling for free use of the library.

His stint as a young man in the family pencil business was peculiar as well. Fearing failure, he made money for the enterprise. Fearing success, he interpreted the experience as a violation of his values. Fearing to stand up to his father, he exasperated him.

Out of step was the way Thoreau marched through life. In the beginning of his association with Emerson he was laughed at for trying to copy his successful friend's speech and mannerisms. He had trouble finding jobs, he had trouble keeping jobs, and his anxiety over this drove him to unscrupulous and irrational behavior. Knowing he would be refused because he lacked the stated qualifications, he applied for a teaching post in Virginia—knowing also that the reply would be slow in coming and that until it came he would appear to family and friends to be looking for work, "waiting to hear." After he actually landed a schoolmaster's post in Concord, the trustees of the school criticized him for being too lenient with students. He accepted this meekly in person but delivered his idea of a counterpunch by beating several children on the eve of resigning. He conducted a courtship in the nineteenth-century hearts-and-flowers style but never married.

It is not clear whether Thoreau was any more reliable as an outdoorsman than as a handyman. His ability to draw out loggers and other rough types, for which his own writings are the main evidence, did not develop by sweating alongside them. In a strange episode in 1844 this master woodsman let a cooking fire get out of control and burned more than three hundred acres of forest. Setting the matter straight to his own satisfaction later in the *Journal*, he remembered "only" one hundred acres, omitted the fact that a number of townspeople called him a damned rascal over the incident, and pictured the fire almost as an artistic creation.

Gradually Thoreau learned how to turn his odd ways into a performance and even intimate that he was in step with celestial rhythms. In his middle years, when he had devised a routine of nature outings, writing, and wangling dinner invitations, he sometimes made day trips into New Hampshire and hiked up Monadnock. Late in the afternoon he would hurry down the south slope to catch the train home to Concord, a make-believe commuter who used a mountainside for his office because he had none in town. He has been called to account by biographers for vanity about a quasi-official position as town surveyor toward the end of his life, but perhaps his satisfaction came from the sheer novelty and blessed relief of doing something normal for once.

Solitude played a different part in Thoreau's life than appears in his books. On ordinary days, when they were busy, people had no time for Thoreau. (He irritated Lidian Emerson by wanting to chat while she did her chores.) But he was the most popular person in Concord for ice-skating parties—his social specialty. His reputation for livening up parlor conversation with eccentric opinions brought him invitations from one class of hosts (although Emerson was sometimes annoyed by Thoreau's habit of arguing the contrary of whatever viewpoint was expressed). Decorous table manners and winning ways with elderly ladies accounted for other invitations. For a man in no position to reciprocate, he dined out often and well. He was assiduous, too, at getting letters of introduction to people he wanted to meet when he traveled, but then tended to talk so much and so ingenuously about himself that they were sorry he had come. Walt Whitman, for example, notoriously tolerant, was put off by him. To Robert Louis Stevenson he seemed "dry, priggish, and selfish." Upon meeting Thoreau in the 1840s, the elder Henry James described him as "the most child-like, unconscious, and unblinking egotist it has ever been my fortune to encounter." James Russell Lowell referred to him as "a little man trotting after Emerson."

The author of *Walden* never lived in splendid isolation beside a wilderness lake, avoiding all truck with money-grubbers and hypocrites. He built his cabin by permission on land owned by Emerson at Walden Pond, where he slept in a bed with sheets. On Saturdays, weather permitting, his mother and sisters brought him cookies and other good things to eat. On Sundays the Walden Pond Society, to which he belonged, organized outings in the area. Picnics were held at his cabin, and as many as twenty-five people crowded inside during rainstorms.

Because he was a writer, Thoreau had a chance to improve the situation. In the flesh: a childish, intelligent, maladjusted, energetic, idle, sensitive, spiteful, and in his way gregarious man. On the printed page: a persona rather more virtuous, consistent, and authoritative than he could manage in life. For readers over the generations to keep company with the figure in the text would benefit more people than for Thoreau to align his contradictions with those of his neighbors. Yet quirks and partly self-inflicted bad luck hampered him as a writer too.

For one thing, his literary taste and talent were probably better suited to the eighteenth century than to his own time. He could not tell a multilayered story or create an atmosphere in which symbols glimmered and resonated as they did for Poe, Hawthorne, and Melville. He was fond of classical literature, and as with Samuel Johnson and other neoclassical writers his best work consisted of single sentences and short passages that could be pulled out to stand alone as maxims and aphorisms.

> Man is rich in proportion to the things he can afford to let alone.

> Fire is the most tolerable third party.

> Beware of all enterprises that require new clothes.

> The youth gets together his materials to build a bridge to the moon . . . , and, at length, the middle-aged man concludes to build a woodshed with them.

> The perception of beauty is a moral test.

Like the propositions of the Federalist Papers, such statements arrive in print as though from eternity—no throat clearing or idiosyncrasy. They are universal statements about "man" and "youth" and "beauty"—as impersonal as Latin mottoes. He might have done better with the pastoral mode if he had treated it in the neoclassical manner: artifice strictly removed from the drudgery of real rustic life. Then there could have been winsome maids and charming swains, gamboling flocks, leafy bowers. Readers would be spared the incongruous mixture of "impervious and quaking swamps" with homespun tips on tying knots and growing beans.

In Thoreau's day, however, tinged with romanticism, writers were under pressure to develop a personal style. The method he chose verged on mechanical, indeed on what today might be called a formula. Emerson noticed this with regard to phrasing. "The trick of his style is soon learned; it consists in substituting for the obvious word and thought its diametrical antagonist. He praises wild mountains and winter forests for their domestic air; snow and ice for their warmth. . . ." Subsequent comparison of Thoreau's manuscripts with his books has revealed an equally mechanical way of building sections and chapters. When an idea with literary possibilities struck him, he would jot it down and file it away. Later, when such notes had been revised and entered in the *Journal*, he would select passages, rework them further, and stitch them together. Incidents that happened years apart or to someone else or only in his imagination, details from scenes collected in the same way, and reflections and sentiments also stored up in advance were combined in the interest of composition. From a large stock of both, he would join a high-minded thought to a particularized scene, as though the thought had occurred on the spot to a reflective and acutely observant philosopher-woodsman as he followed tracks in the snow, say, or watched the sun set over a pond.

Thoreau spent the better part of his life polishing the *Journal*—thousands of pages. A dozen years passed between the writing of the earliest fragment of *Walden* and the writing of the last insertion. He put the book through seven drafts, finishing the bulk of it four years after he returned to his parents' house from the pond. Although the design is plain, Thoreau's writing has the candor of an Oriental rug.

If Thoreau neglected to ground one of his "high" thoughts in the "natural" world, a fatuous dictum could result:

> For every inferior, earthly pleasure we forego, a superior, celestial one is substituted.

If he was careless with natural details, the result could be as ludicrous as one of Fenimore Cooper's Indian speeches. In a poem equating the frontier with bold self-sufficiency, for example, he identified himself with a pine tree whose needles "All to the west incline." P. T. Barnum could have made a tidy sum exhibiting such a tree, its needles growing parallel to the ground and pointing in the same direction from both sides of every branch.

In terms of attracting an audience, Thoreau's literary strategy came near failing. Only two of his books were published in his lifetime, and they were neither prized by the elite on whose fringe he hovered nor widely read. Not all periodical editors disliked him as keenly as Margaret Fuller at the *Dial*, who resented Emerson's intervention on his behalf. None who accepted an essay or two over the years, however, asked him to write regularly for them. His public lectures, meant to produce income and at least a little of the celebrity bestowed on Emerson, were poorly received. Thoreau's dedication to radical causes took place on the sidelines. Neither the public nor officialdom was stung by his objection to the Mexican War and to slavery, and he played no significant part in the organized opposition. Evidently his contemporaries suspected that the "prism of nature" of which he wrote was really a lens through which to magnify their faults for his spiteful satisfaction. In the final year of his life he carpentered a special box for his manuscripts, hoping that posterity would rescue nearly two million words.

The words were saved. In a spirit of antiquarianism and local piety the rest of his books were published in the 1880s and 1890s, and the *Journal* came out in fourteen volumes in 1906. From that point onward, a second phase of Thoreau's relationship to American culture unfolded, one of discovery and canonization at odds with each other.

Discovery proceeded at a time when graduate schools and learned societies were proliferating in the United States. Over the next fifty years an expanding academic system created a relatively large body of specialists in American history and literature. These of course were the very people to assemble evidence about Thoreau, and they found a lot to do. He was, after all, no ancient saint born far away a thousand years ago among credulous illiterates. Besides his own voluminous writings, there were the memoirs and letters of contemporaries. College and town records survived, newspapers and magazines of the time, daguerreotypes and drawings.

What they found—the truth about Thoreau in his original phase—created a problem for the specialists. His make-believe and self-centeredness caused some of them to throw up their hands in disgust. Perry Miller, who edited a previously lost journal for publication in 1958, concluded scornfully that Thoreau's writing was "from the beginning a self-conscious effort to create a 'mythology' out of the village Apollo, Henry Thoreau." "Emerson loved ideas even more than men," wrote Leon Edel, "and Thoreau loved himself." As for social concerns and bold gestures of conscience, Joseph Wood Krutch upon searching the record decided that Thoreau's view—a healthy society is one "in which no part need be taken"—was partly an excuse for doing nothing and partly a defense against the humiliation of being left out.

According to Krutch, Thoreau had no effect on political thought in his day and little subsequently except as a source of rhetoric. Leo Marx, not wishing simply to dismiss as a fraud a figure now prominent in American culture, thought it best to let the life go and stay on the plane of art. "Thoreau restores the pastoral hope to its traditional location," he declared. "He removes it from history, where it is manifestly unrealizable, and relocates it in literature."

The majority of specialists, however, were more inclined to gloss things over, to swallow rather easily the vagaries of a writer, and for a purpose very different from Perry Miller's to point out that it would be unsophisticated to identify the "I" of a book with the author of that book. Professional interest was at stake. The more "classic" American authors, the grander the realm of the specialists. Thoreau was now a source of fundable, publishable projects. Middlemen of culture—journalists, pop biographers, compilers of mass reference books, teachers who neither did primary research nor read secondary sources critically—had even less reason to weigh the evidence. Anything more complicated than a model of self-reliance, literary genius, and clean conscience would spoil their copy.

Ironically, once he was made available through discovery in a cursory sense, remoteness from the world in which he lived helped to win a general audience for Thoreau at last. The population of the country had shifted from farms and villages into cities and suburbs. Relatively few readers knew a fox burrow from a woodchuck hole. They did not notice the absence of manure and infected blisters from Thoreau's scenes. They had no idea that it was impossible to dig a cellar in the time he reported or that, contrary to what he wrote, black flies and no-see-ums do not vanish when the back country is settled. More often than not, readers versed in the natural science of a later day never thought to hold Thoreau accountable as a source of information. They liked the attitude he expressed. Furthermore the preoccupations that the new audience read into Thoreau reflected the acceleration of trends of which he had only an inkling. Readers now confronted alienation, estrangement, rootlessness, broken and lost connections en masse as well as personally. They experienced loneliness in crowds and in a jumble of structures, vehicles, and trash.

On holidays they "viewed" trees and waves as though these were on exhibit in a large zoo. In addition to being comforted by the transcendental belief that nature was benign and just, Thoreau got instant relief from his troubles by retreating to meadows and woods in his immediate vicinity. Latter-day readers had to make do with nostalgia and half-measures for the preservation of a tattered landscape. Whereas much of the energy in his writing came from the frustration and anxiety of not fitting in, such readers interpreted it to express their sense of being imprisoned in offices, streets, and mass institutions.

Nonetheless the combination of selective discovery and craving for relief for reasons the opposite of his raised Thoreau's status. He entered classroom anthologies fairly early in the second phase. Conservationists and those involved in civil rights issues claimed him for their own. A tacit assumption that he was socially safe by those whose power and wealth gave them a disproportionate influence over national image-making cleared the way for him to become a recognizable name in the broader culture. Thus the mid-twentieth-century Thoreau, a source of quotations for editorials, sermons, prefaces, commencement addresses, park dedications, and the like. Though on occasion his words raised the consciousness of suburbanites at the bird feeder a shade too high and made crusaders against phosphate in detergents a tad too vehement, he generally escaped attack during the country's recurrent fits of red-baiting and anti-intellectualism. He was a godsend for teachers: a certified classic author with a relatively simple vocabulary who did not broach sex or other rude topics that would draw the fire of school boards and parents. The portrait of this famous "resister" hung in schools and libraries and eventually appeared on a postage stamp. The second phase transformed him into an emblem of virtue for a wide range of civic purposes.

A third phase of Thoreau's relationship to American culture seems to be under way, in which the virtue attributed to him will be destroyed for private gain. In 1988 one of the largest mutual funds in the United States sought a new gimmick in a campaign to persuade investors who took a beating in the stock market not to withdraw their remaining money. On envelopes for a mass mailing the firm printed the following: "A man is rich in proportion to the number of things he can afford to let alone.—THOREAU." Earlier a paper company with timber holdings the managers had decided not to cut yet because of market conditions quoted Thoreau in advertising themselves as good stewards of the land. To people who commission and produce such junk, the only question is where to find symbols with authority. There are never many at any one time, and as fast as the novelty of perverting them wears off, devaluing legitimate use in the process, they have to be abandoned. Symbols are depleted at least as recklessly as timber and topsoil.

Thoreau's pronouncements on waste, hypocrisy, and money-grubbing turn out to be ironically prophetic. Although his personal chicanery was the merest artistic license compared with the bad faith and false witness of money-grubbers, some of the freshest, most vivid evidence of their dishonesty stems from exploitation of Thoreau himself. Is a moralist so easily implicated in what he condemns to be credited for prescience or debited for lacking sting?

In the first phase an odd and marginal person barely lived down a number of disgraceful episodes. Thoreau pardoned himself for setting the woods afire. He sponged off Emerson. He dressed up walks around the rural block as moral feats. His way of opposing churchiness, the Mexican War, and slavery was bound to be ineffectual: just say no to society. Yet he persisted, stubborn as a mule about presenting himself on his own terms.

In the second phase posterity welcomed Thoreau's celebration of independence. Since the real thing, independence itself, was inadequate to hold a society together and unattainable in a nation filling up with people and machines, symbolic loyalty and enactment had to be the main means for upholding independence as an absolute value. A bold contingent that included Francis Parkman, Owen Wister, and Theodore Roosevelt tried the strenuous life as an alternative, deliberately seeking frontier and cross-class adventures, but they maintained permanent residence in the better part of town and spent a good deal of time celebrating too. Most people necessarily practiced their faith in cramped circumstances, and at this Thoreau had been a master. It propelled him into fame.

Whether readers transformed Thoreau into a stick figure or he constructed a stick figure he knew would appeal to them is a nice question. Even when they are mobilized for enormous collective projects, be it a war to make the world safe for democracy or a war on poverty, Americans lap up sermons on the importance of self-pursuits, and it does not take a supremely smart writer to figure that out. Yet among the prophets of independence Thoreau stands out for lack of interest in violence, real or symbolic, which presumably he knew to be a crowd pleaser too and often intertwined with independence as a cultural theme.

Typical. He wrote his way out of isolation onto common ground, but what he managed to share with the rest of us was a neurotic dread of conformity.

The Case
of the Missing T-Shirt

☼

In 1923, celebrating the newly won right of American women to vote, victorious suffragists arranged to put up a statue of Lucretia Mott, Susan B. Anthony, and Elizabeth Cady Stanton in Washington. When it came to plans for the unveiling, they made a choice that seems remote today but was compelling to those who had fought for the Nineteenth Amendment. They asked Edna St. Vincent Millay to write a poem for the occasion.

The organizers of the event counted on Edna Millay to put a glow into the proceedings. Close up, the voice, the confidence and energy, the remarkable red hair—her aura—often stirred contemporaries. Born in 1892, she had been reading Shakespeare since the age of nine, writing for publication since she was fifteen. A public recitation had prompted a stranger, Caroline B. Dow, to raise money to send her to Vassar, whose president, when he got to know her, predicted that she would accomplish whatever she wished in the world. (Her answer to a question about British colonial policy in her entrance exam for Vassar had concluded with the quip that "it was not a policy at all, just a habit," and she arrived on campus with snowshoes strapped to her luggage.) Sara Teasdale had her up for a talk when she moved to New York. A normally hypercritical professor at Columbia pushed a story of hers into *Smart Set*. To Floyd Dell, an early love, she virtually embodied the slogan of his magazine *The Masses:* "Fun, Truth, Beauty, Realism, Feminism, and Revolution." At a distance too, despite her intellectual pursuits, the organizers could expect journalists and the public to take notice, because she was what they understood in any sphere—a success. "Renascence," the poem that launched her career, was picked for publication from a slush pile of ten thousand manuscripts submitted in a national contest. For *A Few Figs from Thistles*, a book that eventually went through six printings, she had received a Pulitzer Prize the year before the ceremony in Washington, the first won in poetry by a woman. Stupendous praise was laid on her over the years, as when Thomas Hardy, of all people, said that America's two great contributions to the world in the 1920s were "its architectural innovations and Edna St. Vincent Millay."

Better yet for the feminist cause, she more or less consciously used the scandal of a poet's life to publicize the attitude and presence of the New Woman. By 1923 she was reaching restless spirits across the country who would never take poetry itself seriously. To defy stodgy elders and neighbors, they appropriated her line "My candle burns at both ends." Her Nancy Boyd dialogues, collected in a book the year after the suffragist dedication, flouted gender stereotypes and Victorian taboos in passages such as the following: "As for the day we got caught in a shower on Lake George and were obliged to go ashore and seek shelter under the canoe together, I can only say that such accidents happen to us all. I take cold easily. And you were the only dry spot for miles around."

Although her mother, Cora Millay, probably never wrote a manifesto or marched in the streets, Edna was in effect a second-generation feminist. After having three daughters (the first by natural childbirth "for the experience"), Cora divorced her husband, supported the family by hiring out as a practical nurse, and taught her girls serious literature and music—all this in small-town Maine at the turn of the century. By 1910 Cora and her daughters had taken up smoking, and indeed for Saturday night parties at their house they composed a song that included the words:

> Oh, a man is just a man
> But a little old Fatima
> Burns so snug

Norma Millay became a singer, and Kathleen, the other sister, a novelist. When Cora visited Edna in New York in 1918, a first trip to the big city, the older woman immediately had her hair bobbed.

Assertiveness, doubly important to the women's movement to build up morale and overcome resistance, ran in the family, but Edna took it to new heights. As a girl growing up in Camden and other little towns in Maine, she raced the boys at school, climbed mountains, swam in the frigid water of Penobscot Bay, and literally ice-skated in her kitchen when the pipes burst from cold. "I'll slap your face," she responded as a young woman to Arthur Ficke, an established poet whom she then hardly knew, when he asked whether she had borrowed a line from another writer. "I see things with my own eyes, just as if they were the first eyes that ever saw." "I'm getting awfully tired of James Branch Cabell, sentimental old cock," she wrote to a friend. "His books are all alike—the pent-up drool of a long and timorous adolescence." When Edmund Wilson remarked that she had enough ex-beaux to form an alumni association, she shot back (in French), "They always talk about it, but they never do it." In her prime, Millay let it be known that "I want to walk into my dining room as if it were a restaurant and say 'What a charming dinner' "—meaning that someone else, not necessarily female, could damn well shop, cook, serve, and clean up. One of the interesting characteristics of her writing was her ability to turn the patriarchal tone back on men, speaking it as firmly as they did and more suavely. The narrator of "The Concert," for example, insists on leaving her lover at home and reassures him in what might be called a fatherly way:

> Come now, be content.
> I will come back to you,
>   I swear I will;
> And you will know me still.
> I shall be only a little taller
> Than when I went.

In one of the sonnets published in *The Harp-Weaver*, a male character aflutter with the significance of their experience in bed together is told by the woman in the poem:

> I find this frenzy insufficient reason
> For conversation when we meet again.

The conscientious objector in the poem with that title says:

I shall die, but that is all that I shall do for Death;
I am not on his pay-roll.

In a larger sense the choice of Edna Millay by the suffragists continued to be vindicated for the next twenty years or so. *Aria da Capo,* her principal play, was staged under her own direction by the Provincetown Players, premier American theater group of the 1920s, published in a leading literary magazine, and translated into French. *Wine from These Grapes* (1934), her best book of poems, sold forty thousand copies in four months. She wrote the libretto for Deems Taylor's opera *The King's Henchman,* which received a twenty-minute ovation on opening night and was sung at the Metropolitan fourteen times over three seasons. Her solo reading tours made money even during the Depression, and in 1941 RCA asked her to record.

Edmund Wilson, Witter Bynner, and many other writers of her generation remained enthusiastic, and several younger writers acclaimed her. Karl Shapiro in the 1940s, for example, referred to her as "a poet of lyric genius." Louise Bogan, a seasoned editor as well as an accomplished poet in her own right, ranked her "unofficial feminine laureate." Considering that Millay's taste in literature was not really modern and that in middle age she pulled back from literary politics to live at Steepletop (a berry farm in upstate New York), she was reasonably perceptive and generous to other writers in return. When committees and foundations sought Millay's opinion, she gave it in favor of E. E. Cummings, Robinson Jeffers, Leonie Adams, and Kay Boyle. Though she warred with the New Critics and took a silly, petulant tone toward Ezra Pound and T. S. Eliot, she was one of the first in her time to rediscover the poems of John Donne and appreciate the skill of Gerard Manley Hopkins.

Although "scandalous" behavior to promote social causes gradually disappeared from her life after 1927, the year she was arrested in Boston for protesting the execution of Sacco and Vanzetti, she still provided quite a domestic model for feminists. Eugene Boissevain, married to her for twenty-six years, believed her work more important than his, quit the import business, and risked ridicule as a househusband. As a married, middle-aged woman Millay made an issue of registering in her own name at hotels and of skinnydipping when the mood struck her during summers in Maine. The difficult decision in her life, she told a journalist, was not home versus career but poetry versus music. Her sense of sisterhood was still strong as she came to the age when friends begin to die. "Song for a Lute," a sonnet written in memory of Elinor Wylie, opens with the line "Oh, she was beautiful in every part!"

Not only did Millay keep writing, but she grew as a poet. The proportion of flapper wisecracks and pretty descriptions went down. The proportion of lean, sober phrases went up. Lines on the order of "And the weedy rocks are bare to the rain" and "Death beating the door in" emerged. Her power to draw universals from homely particulars increased, as in the following passage from "Childhood Is the Kingdom Where Nobody Dies":

> To be grown up is to sit at the table with people
> who have died, who neither listen nor speak;
>
> . . .
>
> Run down into the cellar and bring up the last jar
> of raspberries; they are not tempted.

She even, if there is such a thing, died becomingly—instantly of heart failure in 1950, after a night of vetting Rolfe Humphries's translation of Catullus. (She was regarded as a first-rate Latinist.)

This is not to imply that Edna Millay was a perfect poet or a perfect feminist. Nor should her life be presented as a fairy tale in which a princess thrives effortlessly for sixty years without pain, failure, blemishes, or enemies. Arthur Ficke, the love of her life, married someone else. Millay endured drastic intestinal surgery, injured her arm and spine when she was thrown out of a car, and suffered two nervous breakdowns. She and Eugene came near being broke during World War II, and she swallowed her share of humiliations. Once when receiving an honorary degree, for instance, she was shut away with the dean's wife and excluded from a faculty convocation to which all the other recipients (male) were welcomed. Though perhaps underestimating the force of oblivion, she realized she had no way to control the future. As she complained in a letter in 1950:

You cannot possibly know what the anthologies are doing to me. What the anthologists of poetry do, naturally, since they are not interested in poetry, interested only in selling their books, is to include the poems which they think will have popular appeal. Of my poetry they like to print such simple and youthful poems as "Afternoon on a Hill" and "Recuerdo" . . . ; and if they use any sonnets, their preference is to use only love sonnets and written in the Elizabethan form.

Nevertheless, Edna Millay was an exceptionally talented and attractive person. Given this knowledge and given current concern with the status of women, wouldn't you expect to find her name on the roster of culture heroines?

Suppose that in 1968 you had volunteered for a mission to Mars and that this year, approaching retirement age, you returned to Earth. After skimming the back issues and mail that piled up while you were in orbit, after feeling your way into current conversations, and after reading notices connected with your pension, insurance, and credit applications, of one thing you would be convinced. Namely, any woman with a public record as impressive as Edna Millay's is bound to figure in feminist posters, slogans, and calendars. If portraits of ancestral heroines decorate the walls at the Fitness and Commodities-Trading Day Care Center, her picture must be there.

Approximately two generations after Millay's heyday, feminism is cresting again, perhaps higher than before. Assertiveness and achievement are high on the agenda. Women executives, women police, women professors, and women athletes command attention. More than ever, efforts are made to correct the womanless history traditionally written by men. Feminist scholars work up dogged studies arguing that female felons of a certain time and place were as crooked or as persecuted as male criminals. Undertones almost of jubilation are detectable when it can be shown that a certain class of women workers had it even worse than downtrodden men. Faculty members in women's studies are driven in particular to prove that women performed competently in arts and sciences for which men said they were unfit. Relics are lovingly uncovered, such as the publication as early as 1566 of music composed by a woman (Madalena Casulana's

Venetian madrigals). Dead male critics are dug up and thrashed for belittling Kate Chopin. A desire for retribution hovers over papers with titles such as "Florida Motifs in the Novels of Constance Fenimore Woolson," which are otherwise lifeless as required by Ph.D. ritual.

Of course at the time you left for Mars, Millay was long dead and virtually forgotten except by American Lit. specialists. But writers' reputations go up and down like the stock market, and in any case it is not necessary to be read to serve as an inspirational figure. After all, this is an age of T-shirts rather than statues. We no longer ration tributes, carve them in stone, and expect perpetual consensus. Just about anyone or anything may serve as a wearable emblem and casually be granted cultural resonance—the Grateful Dead, Pope Paul, Copenhagen Snuff, Wittgenstein, the Second Annual Kansas City Chili Festival. It is no big thing to imprint T-shirts with an image or motto for a picnic or an art fair. Week after week in the back pages of the highbrow periodicals Charlotte Brontë T-shirts, Emily Dickinson T-shirts, and Virginia Woolf T-shirts are advertised.

Oddly enough, however, your guess about Edna Millay turns out to be mistaken. For all practical purposes the "feminine laureate" is still absent. No doubt an entrepreneur somewhere must have tried a Millay T-shirt, but you will not see it on the street. Anthologies and textbooks in which she is nominally preserved now give the impression of including a snippet from her work only because they trade in comprehensiveness. One night when a bunch of the girls are whooping it up at the Malemute Saloon, so to speak, ask what they think of her. Probably you will get blank stares. They don't think of her at all. But if anyone is present who did the "outside reading" several years ago, comments like the following may pop out. "Genteel romantic with a flapper overlay." "Sucked up to men and sold out for a rich husband." "Who needs a poetess!"

Facts, you understand, don't enter into this reaction. An audit would show that on balance it was the other way round: men played up to her. She lived high at times—summers on Ragged Island in Maine and winters in cushy places such as Carmel and Sanibel Island (where she lost a seventeenth-century emerald ring in a hotel fire)—but mostly she paid the bill with her own earnings. Flippant lines, cute lines, and precious lines are on record, but her best work, which is also her late work, is somber. Epithets such as "poetess" hark back to resentment among some of her contemporaries over good luck, celebrity, and kind treatment. Little real animosity lies behind them now, for they have come down third hand, pat responses to her name. No one disputes the facts, because no one cares. The residual folklore about her simply leads in a tight little circle back to the original question. Why are there no Edna Millay T-shirts?

Possibly Millay has to take the blame herself in several respects. She never changed her mind about the capability of women and the independence to which they are entitled. Yet in middle age she seemingly abdicated from making public gestures and jumping into public controversies that might help the cause of women generally. She took on no protégées in her own sphere and showed little interest in strong women such as Eleanor Roosevelt or news photographer Margaret Bourke-White outside it. The "cultural radicalism" of the early 1920s remained her main model, poorly sustained as she grew older and times changed.

The social path Millay chose when she left Greenwich Village distanced her from many concerns of the literary community during the second half of her lifetime. By living in quiet country houses and stopping in comfortable hotels she in effect withdrew from the gossip, exchange of favors, squabbles, and romances through which writers, especially New York writers, cultivate careers. Although she raised money for unemployed actors during the Depression and wrote propaganda during World War II, she paid little attention to Marxism. What might be called the CCNY experience—ethnicity and poverty with cerebration, ruptures over the Moscow Trials, reflections on high culture versus mass culture—was remote to her. She was skeptical of new forms and resistant to treating the act of composition as subject matter—an essential element of modernism in all the arts. To critical theory and the movement of modern literature into the academic curriculum she was indifferent if not hostile. In short she courted obsolescence.

This was quite apparent when she let fly at the stars of modern poetry with no good reason and with no result except to make herself look spiteful and out of touch. "Coarse" and "obscene" were her words for W. H. Auden and Ezra Pound. She carped about T. S. Eliot, labeling him a "death-bringer" and saying, "He has no sense of humor, and so he is not yet a true Englishman." Although womanhood tended to be personally unappetizing to Auden, alarming to Eliot, and distracting to Pound, they were enlightened when measured by standards then prevailing, and it could not help women then to single them out for attack. One of Pound's thousand programs was in fact fully realized by a woman, the poet H. D., whom he befriended, coached, and sponsored. She packed what she deemed to be her master work with, as Katha Pollitt noted in the *New York Times* when the book was reissued in the 1980s, "gnostic, astrological, biblical allusions, crosscultural parallels and large ideas," to which add clinical psychology, ancient mythology, and strategic discontinuity—the sort of erudition Millay believed women should have access to. At least it could do women no good to attack these men in the tone Millay took, which suggested envy and petty malice. As modernist apostles they were cloaked in the dignity of a doctrine that aimed to transcend personal authority. Against them, she gave the impression of someone shooting off her mouth as compared with someone worshipping. The timing of the outbursts was unfortunate too. Since they erupted near the end of her life, they turned out to be exit lines and therefore likely to be better remembered than what she had said and done when she was moving ahead of history.

Still, to dwell on these infractions calls to mind the way in which rape trials have often been conducted—with the victim under suspicion. Circumstances and broad movements over which she had no control worked against her, and somebody, though not the men so far named, was out to get her.

Millay excelled in classical and traditional European forms. Her rendition of a cavalier in "Aubade," for example, is a nearly perfect re-creation:

> From the wound of my enemy that
>   thrust me through in the dark
>   wood,
> I arose with sweat on my lip and
>   the wild wood-grasses in my spur.
> I arose and stood.

> But never did I arise from loving
> her.

How could she prevent the general audience from slipping farther from the feeble grasp of schoolmarms? That audience cherished vernacular themes such as "on the road" and "in the American grain." In ever greater numbers they preferred prose to poetry of any kind, pictures to words, and staging to print. Cavaliers and sprung rhythm were equally unreal to them. As for the special audience of modernists, they put an extreme value on originality. Up-to-date readers expected new forms and confessional poetry. (Louis Simpson, something of a dissenter, once compared twentieth-century American poets' endless examination of self to "a truck spinning its wheels.") This audience could not recognize Millay's work as newly created poetry.

Since she had made waves on behalf of the New Woman, how could Millay foresee that the dosage of titillation and scandal consumed by the public would triple after her time? Had she become spectacularly self-destructive or eccentric, apocryphal anecdotes and warmed-over feature stories might have kept circulating. Had she become monumentally testy as her friend Edmund Wilson did, taking on the Internal Revenue Service and the Modern Language Association in his final years, she might have gained the stature of a counter-institution. Had she lived to an extreme age like Georgia O'Keefe, she might have been patronized as a remarkable survivor and last link with bygone times (in which case the earlier, more adventurous part of her life would be better remembered).

And how could Millay know that the publication of two very tame biographies and a collection of her letters in the twenty years after her death would if anything lower her reputation? In editing the letters, her old friend Allan Ross Macdougall (perhaps influenced by her publisher or executor) included some of the worst mush and gush in the annals of woman. "Mumsie dear" one of them begins (written by her as an adult). "Wumps dear, the little bag is the sweetest bag Sefe ever saw—I am trazy about it," another one says.

More was involved in Millay's obliteration, however, than her quirks, shifts in fashion, and the preoccupation of posterity with itself.

When she snubbed academic critics and casually insulted writers who provided work for explicators, she made enemies.

Modern art and literature had long since become a focal point in a sort of underground communion to compensate for the defects of everyday life in industrial society. As the deepest, richest use of symbols, literature, modern critics argued, embodies an otherwise inexpressible wisdom superior to mere utility. Thus far Millay agreed with them. Through seriousness of perception, they went on to say (rejoicing in the phrase), rapt attention to each text as a formed experience, the critic's priestly role is to mediate between the lay reader and this transcendent wisdom. Here Millay disagreed, and since the sacramental view of literature was leading to moral authority and academic tenure, its promoters did not want a lippy redhead getting in the way.

By and large, modernists of this stripe had their way, and for a long time they carried on a brisk trade in "difficult" literature. Difficult literature is worthwhile, according to their creed, and worthwhile literature is difficult. Ergo, experts must be employed to explain. Naturally the explanations are difficult too, insofar as they partake of transcendent complexity, for which additional explanation by certified experts is the prescribed remedy.

Furthermore, in passing the sacramental critics did explicitly do their part to consign Edna Millay to oblivion. In an influential article in 1937 John Crowe Ransom condemned her with these words: "The modern intellectual field of reference is too wide to be commanded by the innocent female mind." A few years later Allen Tate excommunicated her heartfelt poem on Sacco and Vanzetti by accusing her of arousing "an affective state in one set of terms" in order to give the benefit of it to "an object quite unrelated"—the sin of sentimentality. Although amoral deconstructionism has replaced sacramental close reading, a tradition persists in the critical guild: don't say anything about Millay unless you can say something bad. Recently a well-entrenched scholar in reviewing a new biography of A. E. Housman reached for an example of Housman's crotchets. The old boy, it seems, actually admired what the reviewer labeled "Edna St. Vincent Millay's inane sonnet sequence in *The Fatal Interview*."

But that still does not get to the heart of the mystery. Of course a pre-T-shirt generation of English professors would be sexists as well as critics; and their oldest, most orthodox successors would be also. The peculiarity consists of today's women literary scholars' looking the other way when an old don sneers inane.

Here are some lines from *The Fatal Interview:*

> Heart, have no pity on this house of
>   bone:
> Shake it with dancing, break it down
>   with joy.

Hardly supreme art, but like a good riff in old-fashioned two-beat jazz this perhaps delivered a punch in its time, by playing on the lowlife expression shake it and break it. House of bone could be a bland fancy, or it could resemble a surgeon's steely view of the person. Against the disjunctive, violent, rodomontade language of much modern literature, the passage probably does come off inane. Yet compared with abandon, steeliness, and other pronounced states of being, purely verbal feats are small potatoes. At any rate, professional explicators are never at a loss for words. Why no interest here, in the passage or in the sneer?

When a woman from an earlier generation has sunk so far out of sight, the expertise of women scholars in unearthing lost heroines is a prerequisite for rehabilitation. The possibility of a forgotten figure getting into play again usually depends on someone knowing how and where to look. Since women scholars do know and are in fact frequently engaged in exhumations, Millay appears to be a logical assignment for them. It should be no overwhelming task for the rediscoverers of the First Novelist of Florida to put in a word for a woman once rated as the finest writer of sonnets since Keats.

Thus the clues gathered in the case of the missing T-shirt reflect awkwardly on women literary scholars. Do they calculate that there is nothing to be gained professionally through this throwback poet? Although she is practically forgotten, traces of a reputation for being sentimental and above all passé linger. At times revisionists get credit for boldness and originality by reversing received opinion, but Millay might be a risky choice for a revisionist ploy, giving the dean an easy excuse for labeling the perpetrator "unsound." And are women scholars loathe to come to terms with Millay in private, because of her disdain for their profession? They take great stock in joining a trade association that claims a near-exclusive license to classify, explicate, and evaluate literature. She saw little value in such an association.

Suspicions multiply. Had she been abused by a stepfather, deserted by a husband, mutilated by a doctor, or imprisoned by a censor, would Millay be more acceptable to women scholars? Do women's rights interest them as a cause or as a wedge for cutting themselves a deal?

How dismal to contemplate a women's movement fractured and corrupted to the point where in some respects it resembles the officer corps in a Latin American dictatorship. In the name of liberty a colonel from another province shoots the general or chases him over the border. By liberty the colonel means he is tired of being a henchman. He wants to be supreme commander of robbing peasants and torturing students. He wants his picture in the plaza and his relatives on the payroll. That is exactly what he will get, for a while, and that is more or less what the country will get forever if the future contains Major Juanita Ramirez waiting to make *her* move.

Perhaps henchwoman would be a position of moral grandeur compared with the restricted and humiliating roles traditionally assigned to women. Fair comment. A little sarcasm and irony may be in order to deflate the above caricature of an understandable tendency among all the sexes everywhere for individuals and interest groups to worry about themselves first, their gender cohorts later. It would be a mistake, however, to overlook the cautionary note in this tale of a missing T-shirt. Women as humorless about their careers as the colonel is about the gold braid on his uniform bear watching. For averting their eyes from a spunky poet, those engaged in setting the world straight on the talents of women ought to have a better reason than the desire to be named to academic committees. Those who intend to put women writers on an equal footing with men ought to make a critical judgment of their own rather than look the other way when a senior professor sneers. The bureaucratization of women was not what Edna Millay had in mind.

Lifestyle

Once the Americans had backed into independence by demanding their rights as Englishmen, what next? No one supposed they were immune to the universal passions distinguished by Kant: for possession, for power, and for honor. To fend off anarchy and sustain a workable society they would have to govern and ration those passions, in the process evolving cultural norms that even those who did not benefit immediately or equally would abide by.

Many foreigners and a fair number of ultra federalists did not see how this could be done without the equivalent of nobility as a social principle. Long live King George (Washington). Nobility, after all, had been the linchpin of social order in Europe for a thousand years. It specified rules for membership in the ruling class, designated responsibility by custom and statute, and allocated control over weapons, resources, and symbols around which society was organized. Holiness rivaled nobility in cultural prestige, but the high-born had privileged access to the church. To justify its position, moreover, the aristocracy conscripted language, loading the word *noble* with positive moral connotations. Intermittently at least, Europeans of all classes acceded to a cultural strategy whereby the few lived well for the many.

By the time Tocqueville came to inspect America in 1831, it was obvious that the founding fathers who rejected hereditary titles and official churches had read American conditions and modern conditions astutely. The commercial value of property outweighed "domain," and commercial activity in general, commodities, transport, technology, industry propelled the society. Titles of nobility would have brought civil war instead of order. Government needed functionaries and partisans, not retainers. Instead of dwelling on novelty as such or on the absence of old ways, Tocqueville was interested in how the social system actually functioned. Though American patterns might be peculiar by comparison with historical and world standards, they were, he thought, just as definite as any others. People learned norms while growing up or settling in as immigrants; they held values in common; and they regulated social transactions accordingly.

One thing he discovered was that Americans believed in the possibility and desirability of starting over. Move to a different part of the country, take up a new occupation, begin another family, break old habits and acquire new ones, become best friends with strangers. Besides the ups and downs of wealth and status intrinsic to a commercially frenetic society, in addition to the whirl of fashion and elections, on top of the itch to build new towns and tear up old neighborhoods, they believed on principle that the past could be disregarded and that individuals had a right to redirect their lives.

Over the years this faith in starting over from scratch has fascinated America-watchers. "The stuff of self-improvement manuals generation after generation," writes Frances FitzGerald in *Cities on a Hill*, "is a major theme in American literature." Attitudes toward this trait differ sharply among the reflective. Someone from a country chewed up by history—a hell of prisons and massacres or a decaying society that has carried certain values to exhaustion—might scorn American naiveté and self-indulgence. Yet someone else from the same kind of place might rejoice that at least one lucky nation preserved its innocence so long. One school of social critics might associate starting over with the loneliness, superficiality, and incoherence of American life. Other social critics might point out in good humor that many so-called changes were simply more of the same, grounded as always in human nature. (The student who dominated the radical caucus continues as the lawyer hell-bent on becoming a partner in the firm.) The especially optimistic and tolerant might hail the latitude to start over as freedom not available in hidebound societies. Still other observers might be struck by paradoxes—a tradition of the new, unanimous individualism. Whatever the attitude, the fact is not in dispute. Americans and to a lesser extent people in all highly industrialized societies tend to believe they can shuck off the past and make new lives.

During the 1970s a word came into common use that perfectly encapsulates this cultural assumption and the social patterns related to it. *Lifestyle* is the word. It was a brave word at first, hinting at rich possibilities, a broad view of human development and the life course, an order that fulfilled rather than constricted. Unfortunately, however, journalists, salesmen, and pop psychologists trivialized it even more rapidly than usual. *Lifestyle* already stands mostly for the section of the newspaper that runs recipes for pumpkin mousse and tips on buying a futon. It sets a pseudo-classy tone when movie actresses on talk shows reveal that they own a dog. Encouraged by an interviewer to think big, a doctor in Boston recently recommended "lifestyle changes such as . . . seatbelt use."

In the short interval before it was trivialized, *lifestyle* sounded more impressive than older terms from the same cultural cluster—terms such as *moving on* and *self-help*. People who could barely count change from a five-dollar bill had fantasies of designing and redesigning their precious selves as Picasso would approach a blank canvas. Partly the pretentiousness of the word resulted from rhetorical battles of the times in which it came into use. But partly it reflected the decline of a countervailing norm that had set limits to the idea of styling oneself.

In place of the hereditary rank they refused to tolerate, Americans at the outset installed respectability as a social anchor. It held in check notions of starting over and anything goes. Achievement and character across class, occupation, gender, and ethnic identity were measured by respectability for two centuries. It lasted as a norm through industrialization, depression, and war.

The generation that came of age about the same time as lifestyle probably cannot fathom the hold respectability once had on the whole society. The better educated and more affluent members of that generation are used to a portfolio mode of culture. Sell migrant workers and buy the homeless. Keep an eye on the greenhouse effect for potential growth in the environmental sector. As safe investments with a steady yield, beer and exercise are dependable. College degrees are down slightly. The only widely shared conception of the common good now is sufficient order and support so that trading may continue. Poorer members of the same generation are necessarily more limited in their options, but they make numerous choices in a volatile market too. Should they dye their hair blue or orange? Should they go for a continuance or a plea bargain?

By the time Elliott Gould, smiling sweetly and wearing a ratty football jersey, was allowed to tell a national television audience that he was glad to host "Saturday Night Live" because the program, in his words, "has balls," a certain number of viewers were titillated, a large number could take it or leave it, and those who were offended had a subconscious suspicion they might be cranks. Just a few years earlier Richard Nixon, villainous and squirrely as they come, had stuck his neck out ten times farther than Elliott Gould; but he was older, and he by god wore a suit, pressed and buttoned, even to board a private airplane. Millions upon millions of decent citizens, beside themselves with anger, fright, and shame, would have been ready to join a lynching party had Gould broken the taboo in 1860 or 1960.

To reinforce the point, against Gould's show-biz effervescence can be set a humorless passage from the Judgment Day section of James T. Farrell's *Studs Lonigan*, received as incendiary realism when it was published in the 1930s. In this scene a housewife with a baby is about to take on four strangers for $2.50 each to recoup the grocery money she lost to a bookie. When Studs draws high card for first turn with her and one of the others says "Leave a little for us," she becomes indignant. "This is my house," she snaps. "Get out if you're going to talk lewd." As the example suggests, respectability extended far beyond the bourgeoisie. Forty years after Studs's fictional lesson in etiquette the historian Tamara Hareven interviewed former workers at the Amoskeag mill in New Hampshire, in its day the largest textile plant in the world under one roof. Virtually every one of them avoided "off-color" talk, though these men and women left school early and were poor all their lives.

Of course youngsters did learn the underground language by hook or crook. Taboos have to do with the forbidden, not necessarily with the unknown. Some of them, on the sly, managed a passable imitation of the toughest kid in town, destined to go directly from grammar school to prison. The boys often encountered an authority —a straw boss, a coach—who used rough language that impressed them. Later, facility in the other language might come in handy for coping with or surviving among troops, laborers, tenants. Going to barrooms, brothels, pool halls, and cooch shows meant having your cake and eating it too: upholding the norm by breaking taboos in a place prescribed for that purpose. Usually by a more subterranean route girls arrived at an equivalent "secret" knowledge, though in some ways a worse state of duplicity.

It would be a great mistake to shrug respectability off as antiquated taste, hypocrisy, and squeamishness. As industrialization proceeded, roles multiplied, population grew, and science put custom into question, something was needed to encourage compliance among segmented, atomized citizens. For stratified democracies and administered authoritarian states, respectability filled the bill. It suited conditions. It worked.

To spend one's life laying trolley track or packing mothballs did not preclude wearing a starched collar on Sunday and subscribing nominally to "clean living," "proper behavior." Such behavior could be demanded by the eminently respectable from the barely respectable, or it could be rewarded with token esteem (address the washerwoman as "Mrs." and share her disapproval of spitting). According to current needs for cheap labor, dirty work, scapegoats, and disenfranchisement, the line could be redrawn expediently at the bottom, denial of respectability justifying discrimination practiced against minorities, immigrants, and subjugated peoples.

In societies composed largely of peasants and artisans, any deliberate departure from pomp had been a manifestation of privilege by other means. This was obvious when ladies of the French court played at being milkmaids or when English peers paraded in public "drunk as lords." As Sartre pointed out, when Saint Francis handed back his clothes to the well-to-do father who had paid for them, the gesture was a moral luxury. The majority around him had no choice but to go ragged and dirty. As per capita income rose and the number of "things" commonly owned increased in industrial societies, downward departures took on a different meaning. In their way—with pearl stickpins, donations to the church, and the like—even hustlers, gangsters, and fixers followed the code of respectability. Out-groups such as Gypsies and circus performers, as well as occupational groups remote from centers of respectability (such as cowboys, loggers, and sailors) were clearly exceptions, rare and exotic. By the same token, however, it was now easy to make dissident gestures against respectability.

Bohemians, on the whole sufficiently educated and sufficiently employable for respectability had they the inclination, in fact made an issue of rejecting it in the conviction that they knew better than respectables how to live. They ranked themselves as aristocrats of the spirit, the elite few with intellect, imagination, taste, and moral courage. Sometimes aestheticism swayed bohemia. The cultivated dandy appeared more debonair, witty, knowing, and above all interesting than any solid citizen. At other times antimaterialism dominated bohemia. Dull respectables who cared about napkin rings and baths were ridiculed and despised. At still other times a "wild" mode ruled bohemia—drugs, outlandish costumes and couplings, links with the underclass, living on the edge.

For a long while a standoff prevailed. On the one hand, enclaves opposed to or opposed by the respectable were often cordoned off—bohemian quarters, shanty towns, red-light districts, and the like. News from the forbidden zone reached ordinary people largely through stereotypes supplied by journalists, dramatists, politicians, and do-gooders—stereotypes of long-haired artists, bomb-throwing reds, Wild West outlaws, scarlet actresses, rascally sporting men, et cetera. Sustained, deliberate counter-respectability rarely presented itself in the barnyard, the mill, the shop, the school, or the social call. On the other hand, crossing the line for pleasure or profit was not too difficult. Novelists did it. The police did it. Real estate operators did it. Dancehalls and casinos lay close to the border. A majority accepted respectability in principle and upheld it or cheated as circumstances dictated. With the cooperation of his sisters and servants, Emily Dickinson's brother, a prominent lawyer and treasurer of Amherst College, managed discreet trysts in the family dining room, which had a large fireplace and a stout door. From roughly World War I forward, furthermore, a resourceful speakeasy mentality helped to preserve the standoff. The cocktail party, the smart set, and cafe society accommodated "nice" people. Blues became "entertainment." The mass media upgraded notoriety to celebrity. True, psychoanalysis showed respectability in an ambiguous light. Revolutions, anticolonial movements, and totalitarianism shook the whole world, and economic depression and another cataclysmic war hit the United States directly. Nevertheless a socially intelligible balance held through the 1940s and 1950s. Mom and Apple Pie, God and Property continued to receive their due. Cultural instructions remained clear: get a haircut, be on time, carry proper identification. Yet room was left to relax—to become temporarily a watered-down Rimbaud, make-believe hoodlum, or attenuated carnival dancer—without losing the thread. It was believed—indeed hoped—that movie stars had orgies galore, preferably on bearskin rugs. The few should live licentiously for the many. But the stars were expected to support the Code of Decency by day and pull the shades at night.

In short, respectability was a strong norm. It had stamina, manipulative power, coherence, and flexibility. And it is not dead yet. A "respectable" way to behave endures, fuzzy and precarious, residually enforceable at law, more or less adhered to by the executive class and the old blue-collar class, deeply ingrained in many families. Numerous "mature" men would still be mortified to appear sockless in public, and numerous women would feel disgraced by a loud belch. By the 1980s, however, respectability was simply a prominent norm in a boutique of norms. No explosion occurred if someone attended the symphony in jungle pants or showed up wearing a "gay" earring to sign a mortgage. People said *lifestyle* without a second thought.

Just as real wars frequently end with both sides worse off than they were before, so lifestyle is the uncomfortable and in the long run probably untenable outcome of the cultural wars of the 1960s and 1970s. Relatively disorganized, formerly unrecognized groups in that period learned to use nonconformity to wage politics. Countercultural presence was shaped to make demands: stop the war, jobs for blacks, power to sisterhood. Rather quickly cultural politics became an issue in itself. For a brief time one could call the Beatles lower-class deformed (as Malcolm Muggeridge did) with only music in mind. Soon those became fighting words. Respectables were held responsible for induced poverty, racism and sexism, stifling routines and alienating work, for police brutality, a vile war in Vietnam, and piling nuclear weapons on each other fifty times over, for shoddy goods, phony sentiments, and crooked deals, for miseducation and the destruction of the environment—in short for the worst of human nature and an intrinsically defective way of life. As this message registered, a great many old believers felt equally hostile and betrayed. Respectability had been painfully drilled into them, they had mastered the whole complicated code and strained to live up to it, and suddenly a crowd of young nobodies, pointy-headed intellectuals, and "agitators" seized the cultural initiative. As they saw it, respectability was being sold out for nothing worth having—drugs, shoplifting, herpes simplex, a rising rate of youthful suicide, and weakness in the face of a Red Peril and a Yellow Peril. Aside from damage done in the famous campus "disruptions," some serious force was used by both sides. The Weathermen, for example, broke windows and beat up professors, and urban rioters torched their own neighborhoods. National Guardsmen gunned down students at Kent State, and police in Berkeley blinded a painter with shotgun fire during the Battle of the People's Park. Symbolism was the common weapon, though. On the one side, students with draft deferments and job prospects burned the flag. Movie actresses—of the type who previously sanctified the status quo by stepping out of limousines in sheath dresses under blue and rose spotlights—appeared with kinky hair, breasts dangling under worn T-shirts. Young ministers offered public prayers for Patty Hearst and her "associates" in the spirit of cheerleaders. On the other side, negotiating and conceding details of respectability so as to guard more important levers of power, the established order cranked out new merchandise: rolling papers, water beds, tape decks, mountaineer packs, socially significant overalls. Rules were dropped, and ways were found to loosen up at a safe distance from hippies, radicals, and poor people. Off with the white shirts, you swinging dentists of

Cherry Hill. On with the doubleknits and the psychedelic ties a yard wide (in what clothing manufacturers around 1970 called the Peacock Revolution). Hoist skirts and tighten jeans across the butt. Put on the gold chains of a good-doing pimp and his teenage whore. Pass for a hip comedian, a centerfold sexpot, a person who sings at Mafia hotels. In the end the result of the cultural battling and of the dispersion of the counterculture was a social type nobody liked: Yuppies. Those who grew up under respectability but were critical of it and hoped attacks on it would lead to a freer, happier, more just society saw their movement trivialized and half-forgotten. Those who defended respectability and hoped for full restoration found themselves living in a cultural boutique among institutions of impaired legitimacy.

Defective institutions such as the multiversity persist. To them have been added greater national inequality and idiotic policies such as prosperity through debt. Non sequiturs are now the staff of life: commodities trading Monday through Friday and gathering wild foods on the weekend; gay liberation and campaigning to return to the Mass in Latin; computer programming to produce astrological charts; save the whales and serve sashimi. With all the jogging and hopping and weight-lifting, whole neighborhoods have been changed into giant track-and-field events, and yet at home the "athletes" use remote-control buttons to change TV channels. Respectability has become an option, part of a jumbled social landscape through which individuals thread their way according to whim and circumstance. The 4-H club need never confront the meditation society, and neither need confront the single-parents group. Roles coexist and succeed each other without adding up.

Among those old enough to view the lifestyle era as a phase, attitudes differ. Some resist, holding on as tightly as possible to what they were comfortable with in the first place—respectability or principled opposition to respectability. They assume the storm will pass, and afterwards an equilibrium such as they remember between social stability and the urge to start over will reemerge.

Doubtful. The adulteration of the counterculture is not to be taken lightly. Now the future is partly in the hands of someone to whom lifestyle is not just a catchword. Farrell's horseplaying housewife had a grandson. Barry, age thirty-two, lives in Houston, where he works for a real-estate trust that manages shopping malls. To him lifestyle is the sea in which he swims, as it is for his sister, who stayed in Chicago and became one of the first women hired as a sales representative in the wholesale wine business. He considers himself to be a regular member of society, in that sense respectable. Yet his world tips in a different direction from that of his grandmother. He comes home at no particular hour, throws his jacket on the floor, says the day was a pisser, throws his mail on the floor, wonders whether to stay in, throws a towel on the floor. After a meal which might or might not be known as dinner and which could equally well include a fast-food gristleburger or fresh-made pesto, he listens inattentively to a tape by the Booger Eaters, skims an article on tax shelters, and during the late news on TV comes to a consensus with one or more people who live with him for the time being that the telephone company sucks, the weather sucks, and Iran sucks.

History separates this man from his grandmother as evolution positions two species to receive light from different regions of the spectrum. *Don't talk lewd.* She clutched at that even while taking on the neighborhood. Respectability was the code her culture trained her to rely on, as it was the code whose infringement made her feel the situation in which she found herself was a crisis. Her grandson has no special talent for breaking taboos or expanding consciousness. He will not directly test the established order's capacity to deflect and absorb. He will probably wear shined shoes if he has to go to court. Yet he may be ultimately unreachable by both respectables and their traditional opponents. How much reality can he ascribe to a norm that for him has no interior?

The question of who he was in a previous existence currently interests Barry. Next year it may be kayaks. Instead of deploring and resisting this lifestyle mentality, part of the older population joins in and counts on it functioning indefinitely. It suits rejuvenation schemes and dreams. Yet their assumption, the opposite of those waiting for the storm to pass, is doubtful too.

Trivial productions do not necessarily have trivial results. Lifestyle clashes with certain deepseated and more important Western ways that are still very much in force. The notion is in the air that out of countless personal preferences will somehow flow public good—pushed along by an invisible hand such as Adam Smith imagined. In a distorted way this continues a Western tradition of individualism: choice, conscience, assent, will as a faculty of self, values created rather than granted. But it is hard to think of a social configuration up to now that makes no provision for relating the individual to a cosmos and a community. How is it possible for humans to live in groups and not share values? When lives are styled in the same space, what keeps them from tangling? To say that at present we can't agree on a reason for human association in the public realm implies that explosive pressure for a new connection will build up.

For good or bad, Western culture has fostered linear thinking. It is embedded in concepts such as prime mover, cause and effect, means and ends, input and output, critical mass, formative stages. It is embedded in proverbs and literature and commerce and science. As the twig is bent, so grows the tree. You can't teach an old dog new tricks. The child is father to the man. Must have successful track record. Rate of return on investment. Relative contribution of nature and nurture. It is bound to be unsettling to move daily between those assumptions and the idea that a life consists of styles that can be chosen, altered, discontinued at will, and replaced like fabrics.

Perhaps the greatest pressure for a cultural framework more settled than lifestyles arises from the strain of assembling the world from moment to moment, like walking a long distance by reinventing the step every two and a half feet. We endure and participate in a welter called experience. The categories into which we divide the welter—such as forces, conditions, stimuli, intervals, feelings, perplexities, and relationships—are not exhaustive and do not necessarily express fact or wisdom in an absolute sense. They simply organize our experience, and thus they are largely worthless if used capriciously.

The advantage of organizing experience on the biological level is clear. Every organism has a genetic program, capabilities fitted to an environment, patterned relations with others of its species, and a boundary (such as skin) to regulate inflow and outflow. Perception automatically sorts experience: focusing attention, triggering response, and enabling skills to develop.

That culture continues in this direction is obvious—economizing effort, standardizing encounters, pooling experience. Thus existence under the dispensation of lifestyles becomes jittery. It is exhausting to hew selves and connections over and over. It is intolerable to have to make up rules each time for each set of social transactions. If nothing else, a culture ought to provide points of reference in a whirling world.

Index

Academic culture, 55, 99–101, 112–13, 127, 128, 129
Akkadian language, 14–15, 16, 22
American culture: adversarial relations within, 6; incoherence of, 95; paradoxes of, 96–106 passim, 113–14, 116, 131–32, 138; role of writer in, 102–6 passim; belief in starting over, 106, 131–32; in an age of T-shirts, 123, 137; conflicts during 1960s and 70s, 136–37
Aron, Raymond, 54
Assyria, 14–18 passim
Ayer, A. J., 61, 71–72, 81

Babylonia, 15–19 passim
Barzun, Jacques, 58
Baudelaire, Charles, 68
Benda, Julien, 58
Bernard, Saint, 45
Bohemians, 54–55, 135
Boissevain, Eugene, 120
Brazil, 28

Chang Kwang-chih, 14
Chavez, Cesar, 85, 86
China: ancient, 14; modern, 38, 50–51; scholar-gentry in, 59, 62–64
Chomsky, Noam, 60, 76, 78–79
Civilization: as organizational revolution, 11–12; Eastern, 12–13; Western, 13, 15, 140

Cooper, James Fenimore: awkward writing of, 96–97, 100; inventor of Western, 97, 99, 106; as social theorist, 101; social background of, 102–3; loss of readers, 105; conservatism in old age, 106
Critics, literary, 79–80, 99–101, 127–28
Culture: embedded in language, 6; diversity of, 11, 12; configuration of, 23; participatory, 24, 36–37; change in, 69, 140. *See also* Academic culture; American culture

Dell, Floyd, 117
Derrida, Jacques, 79
Despotism, 13, 51–52
Dictionary of Americanisms. See Mathews, Mitford
Doolittle, Hilda (H. D.), 125
Dorr War, 88–90

Edel, Leon, 112
Emerson, Ralph Waldo, 80, 96, 107–12 passim

Farrell, James T., 133
Faustian legend, 40
Feudalism: origin of term, 25–26, 28; misunderstood in developing countries, 27–28, 38; Japanese form of, 28–29; productivity of, 28–30, 35–36;

Feudalism (*continued*)
family as economic institution in, 30–32; and contractual relationships, 34–35; and economic mobility, 37–38; scientific activity within, 39–40. *See also* Heresy
Ficke, Arthur, 119, 121
FitzGerald, Frances, 131
Foucault, Michel, 73, 93
Francis, Saint, 134
Franciscans, 34, 43
Free Speech Movement, 85, 90, 92

Gould, Elliott, 133

Hemingway, Ernest, 70
Heresy: loss of its meaning, 42–43; Socinian, 43; Donatist, 44; Hussite, 44–45; Waldensian, 45–46; three aspects of, 45–47; Amaurian, 46; logic of spiritual monopoly, 47–52; its nonexistence in Islam, 48; and inquisitorial posturing, 48; Joachite, 67
Herlihy, David, 30–31
Holton, Gerald, 65
Housman, A. E., 127
Hus, Jan, 47

Intellectuals: as heroic outsiders, 53–55; as intelligentsia, 55; as brain workers, 56; as mandarins and experts, 57–58; as a character type, 64–65; as language purists, 70–73

James, William, 14, 68, 76

Kant, Immanuel, 53, 66, 77, 130
Kolakowski, Leszek, 64
Krutch, Joseph Wood, 112–13
Küng, Hans, 42–43
Ku Yen-wu, 63–64

Lamberg-Karlovsky, C. C., 14
Language, 7–9; drift, 41–42, 59, 93–94; traditional view of 66–68, 77; distrust of, 68–76, 78–79; disposable, 74; in form of social noises, 74–75; relativism, 76–77; situational, 81–82. *See also* Akkadian language
Lawrence, D. H., 99
Lawrence, Mass., textile strike, 85–86, 87
Layard, Henry, 16
Lewis, Bernard, 48
Liberal: as situational word, 81–82
Lifestyle: in Toynbeean sense, 12; as personal choice, 132; and respectability, 132–36; and instability, 136–40
Logical positivism, 8. *See also* Language, distrust of
Lurie, Alison, 102

Marinetti, Emilio, 58
Marx, Leo, 113
Mathews, Mitford, 1–9
Mesopotamia: as locus of Western ways, 14–15; politics and technology of, 16–17; pluralism of, 17–23; social reciprocity in, 23; participatory culture in, 24
Millay, Cora, 118
Millay, Edna St. Vincent: praise of, 117–18; as New Woman, 118, 126; girlhood of, 119; poetry of, 119–21; *Wine from These Grapes*, 120; marriage of, 120, 125–26; in middle age, 120–21; as enemy of modernists, 124–25; neglected by women scholars, 128–29
Miller, Perry, 112, 113
Mitchell, Richard, 76
Mohicans, 97–98

Near Eastern Breakout, 14
Neolithic revolution, 11
Nietzsche, Friedrich, 69, 73
Nobility, 130–31

O'Connor, Frank, 7
Oppenheim, A. Leo, 16

Peters, Edward, 45
Plato, 62
Pluralism, 13–24 passim
Poirier, Richard, 80
Provincialism, temporal, 5–6

Ransom, John Crowe, 127
Reagan, Ronald, 82
Reform: as situational word, 82, 83–84; credentials of reformers, 82–83; attitude of conservatives and radicals toward, 83–84; nonrecognition of, 85–86, 87–90; punishment and appropriation for, 90–93; Age of, 94
Regulators, War of the, 90–92, 93
Rémy, Nicholas, 59
Revolutionary: as situational word, 42, 82
Richards, I. A., 79
Roger of Hoveden, 47
Rome, 24, 29–31
Roszak, Theodore, 58
Russell, Bertrand, 72
Russia: moral authority of writers, 51–52; locus of intelligentsia, 55

Sapir, Edward, 76–77
Sartre, Jean-Paul, 134
Scholes, Robert, 80
Science, 40, 65, 67, 68, 72
Shalamov, Varlam, 51–52
Shen Kua, 59

Shugg, Roger, 2, 5
Simpson, Louis, 126
Socrates: as legend, 53, 59–60; as reactionary, 60–61; as schemer, 61–62, 65
Spiller, Robert E., 99, 101
Stone, I. F., 61
Structural linguistics, 78
Sumerians, 14–16, 22

Tammany politics, 86, 89
Tate, Allen, 127
Thoreau, Henry: as an emblem of virtue, 9, 113–14; his failure to fit in, 107–8, 111–12; as freeloader, 109; writing method of, 109–11
Tocqueville, Alexis de, 130–31
Tyler, Parker, 54

Underwood, Congressman Oscar W., 92
University of Chicago Press, 1–5

Veblen, Thorstein, 95

Wang Hongwen, 50–51
Webster, Daniel, 98
Whorf, Benjamin, 76–77
Willey, Gordon, 14
Wilson, Edmund, 99, 119, 120, 126
Wittgenstein, Ludwig, 72, 123